FINISHING TOUCHES

Jessica Ridley

Charles Scribner's Sons
New York

Author's Acknowledgments

I would like to thank everyone at Colefax and Fowler and,
in particular, George Oakes for teaching me how to paint;
my mother and the rest of my family for their support;
David Fletcher, James Stourton, Mr. and Mrs. Hugh Sackville West,
all at 15 Savile Row and Catherine Bennett for letting me loose in
their houses and allowing me to experiment on their furniture;
Deborah Elliott for testing the recipes and confirming that
the painted finishes can be achieved without previous experience;
Norman Brand, the photographer, for his unfailing good humor;
John Meek, the art editor, for his taste, patience and
attention to detail; and lastly Robert Sackville West,
my editor, for his enthusiasm and encouragement.

Copyright © 1988 by Toucan Books Ltd.
Text copyright © 1988 by Jessica Ridley

Charles Scribner's Sons
Macmillan Publishing Company
866 Third Avenue, New York, NY 10022
Collier Macmillan Canada, Inc.

Library of Congress Cataloging-in-Publication Data

Ridley, Jessica.
Finishing touches/Jessica Ridley.
p.   cm.
ISBN 0-684-19025-7
1. House painting—Amateur's manuals. 2. Interior decoration—
Amateurs' manuals.   I. Title.
TT323.R53 1988
747—dc19   88-17580
                                                          CIP

Bulk purchases of Macmillan books are available at special discounts
for sales promotions, premiums, fund-raising, or educational use.
For details, contact:

Special Sales Director
Macmillan Publishing Company
866 Third Avenue
New York, NY 10022

10 9 8 7 6 5 4 3 2 1

Typeset by Florencetype Ltd, Kewstoke, Avon
Printed in West Germany

CONTENTS

AUTHOR'S INTRODUCTION TO THE ART OF THE PAINTED FINISH

I CAME to the studio at Colefax and Fowler with no art-school training and no experience of even the most basic of decorative painting techniques. And yet within a few weeks of starting work—simply undercoating and sanding furniture—the possibilities suddenly opened out to me. I realized that you could transform the most ordinary piece of wood, for example, into a smooth, luxurious surface, a minor triumph of *trompe l'oeil*.

Since then, I have coached people in the same studio and have begun to appreciate, on the one hand, the difficulties of the various techniques and, on the other, the delight of overcoming them. Most people have some flair for painting and an eye for color that needs only a little encouragement.

The chances are that you too have talent, enthusiasm and ideas. The aim of this book is to provide a practical starting point for developing them. The step-by-step instructions guide you through a range of objects and techniques. Feel free to adapt them as you want and remember that, because you are using oil colors, any mistakes can immediately be wiped away. Miracles will not happen overnight but when, for example, the first person touches a fireplace that you have marbled to check whether it is as cold as the real material, you will realize that you have done a thoroughly professional job.

The first step is to search for inspiration for different effects. Most of the best and seemingly original ideas for painted finishes are taken from existing pieces of furniture or they are inspired by nature. So, don't be afraid of copying; call it adapting, instead. Craftsmen through the centuries have done just the same, so why shouldn't you?

The painted furniture of today has evolved from a long tradition of well-established techniques. Many of these have become so stylized that the finished effect bears little resemblance to the original natural source of inspiration. For example, when you marble or wood-grain an object, you are not trying simply to ape nature; you are also practicing a craft that is centuries old and creating an effect that is sanctioned by the conventions of decorative art. Faux bamboo does not look much like real bamboo; and yet since the 18th century, when the fashion for chinoiserie arrived in Europe, craftsmen have been developing their own interpretation of the real thing which now stands up for itself as a recognized decorative technique. See yourself as perpetuating a great tradition and make the most of what has gone before.

Collecting colors and patterns from old pieces of painted furniture and from nature is a good way to begin. You can take your inspiration from actual pieces of furniture in museums, galleries and antique shops or from photographs in auction catalogs, magazines and books.

Wood is everywhere around the house, and samples are readily viewable at lumberyards. Marble can be obtained from marble warehouses, and suppliers will often provide you with samples of the different types available. All sorts of public buildings, from churches and cathedrals to town halls, feature blocks of marble which you can study. Look, too, in bathroom and kitchen shops for samples. Tortoiseshell is another beautiful surface that is most often found today on small objects such as old hair-brushes and combs. Ideas for stenciling are all around you—from the pattern of an iron railing to the daisies stitched on a Victorian sampler. Any object with a simple design or period feel, often used in a rustic setting, adapts well to stenciling. Cut out pictures or take photographs of anything you like.

The next step is to find an appropriate object on which to apply your ideas. Consider the basic style and shape of anything before you decide on a painting technique. There will, of course, be some objects with design faults that will not be helped by decoration or some techniques that will look odd when applied to incongruous objects: a modest kitchen chair, for example, painted to look like black marble or lapis lazuli. In general, flat-surfaced, square-edged objects lend themselves best to marbling whereas anything cylindrical or tubular, from the back of a chair to a bicycle frame, can be "bambooed." Even the most boring plastic frame or shelf can be wood-grained.

Using traditional techniques and materials for painted furniture may sound rather a performance. The paints are expensive and, because you have to wait a day between each coat of paint, the process takes time. But, in the long run, it is worth it. You can create any effect and color from a limited range of oil-based paints. These traditional paints go a surprisingly long way and are more hard-wearing than modern acrylic or water-based paints. You will quickly become acquainted with the properties of each paint and learn how to exploit them. They also allow a greater margin for error. Because each coat takes a day to dry, you can always wipe away anything with which you are not completely satisfied; with fast-drying modern paints, on the other hand, you either have to live with your mistakes or scrub very hard indeed.

Traditional paints give the satisfaction of lasting longer. But, above all, they are more straightforward and honest. When you paint with them, you can content yourself with the idea that the great artists worked from a limited palette too.

Getting ready

ONE of the joys of adopting traditional techniques in decorative painting is that you need a remarkably limited amount of equipment. The photograph on this page shows all the materials and tools required to accomplish any of the painted finishes in this book. They are available from artists' or decorators' suppliers or from hardware stores.

Materials (from left to right)
- White semigloss paint
- Linseed oil
- Mineral spirits
- Gold size
- Designer's color or gouache
- Acrylic gloss medium and varnish
- Gold leaf
- Fine-surface wood filler
- Eggshell or gloss varnish
- Metal primer
- Flat white paint
- Oil colors (lemon chrome, crimson, cadmium scarlet, burnt umber, burnt sienna, viridian, raw umber, ultramarine, raw sienna, black)

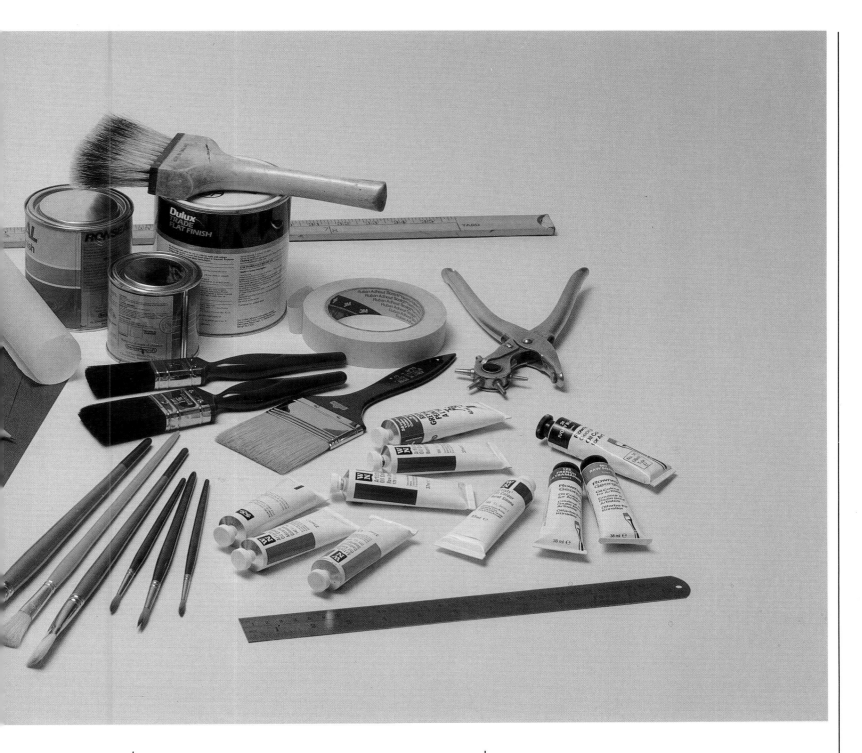

Tools (from left to right)
- Ruler
- Pair of scissors
- Stencil brush
- Mixing brush
- Fan brushes
- Scalpel or craft knife
- Sandpaper
- Stencil paper
- Goose feathers
- Pencils
- Sponge
- Tracing paper
- Fitch brushes (No. 8 and No. 10)
- Sable brushes (No. 4, No. 5 and No. 7)

- Decorator's brushes (1 inch and 1½ inch)
- Flat glazing brush
- Badger softener brush
- Masking tape
- Hole punch

Oil colors

The basic range of ten oil stainers, when mixed together, produces a wide variety of colors. These paints are tough and easy to work with. So long as the surface of the object to be painted has been properly prepared and undercoated, any decorative finish which has been well varnished will last for many years.

As well as mixing with each other, oils are used in combination with flat white paint and varnish. It is, in fact, far better to use them with a medium rather than on their own, as this gives them body and makes them easier to work with over large areas. If you use oils on their own, it is difficult to avoid a streaky and uneven finish and the paints take even longer to dry.

Treat the paints well, putting the tops back onto the tubes, and they will go a long way. Always break the pigments down on the side of a plate with an old brush (rather than your best sable) before mixing them into a glaze.

White

You will need two main types of white: flat and semigloss paint. Flat white is both a basic undercoat and a medium for the glaze. Its purpose as an undercoat is to raise the grain of the wood ready for sanding. Semigloss gives a sheen half way between flat white and gloss. It provides a better key for the glaze than gloss, which dries to such a shiny and slippery finish that a glaze is liable to crack or chip. Semigloss is easily tinted with oil colors, but do make sure that the pigment is thoroughly broken down to avoid dark streaks when you apply the paint.

Mineral spirits

This is the solvent for all the oil paints. It thins them down and can be used for removing them altogether if necessary. Mineral spirits clean grease and dirt from surfaces prior to painting and dry in a few minutes. When adding mineral spirits to paint, always stir it in well to achieve a uniform consistency. In marble finishes, you use mineral spirits on the tip of a feather to cut through the glaze back to the undercoat. This produces a veined effect. A final, and most important, use is for cleaning brushes after painting. Scrub the paint out of the bristles with mineral spirits before washing them in soap and water.

Linseed oil

This has the opposite effect of mineral spirits; it slows down, rather than accelerates, the drying process. If you want to keep a glaze "open" or workable for slightly longer, add linseed oil—but not too much or the mixture will become difficult to control and look greasy and shiny. A few drops should be enough.

Varnish

Varnish comes in three finishes: matt, eggshell and gloss. Although varnish acts primarily as a transparent protective coat to the paint beneath, it can be used as a medium for oil colors. Eggshell gives a gentle sheen, but you may prefer gloss in some cases for a very shiny finish. Varnish dries quickly—taking 4–6 hours per coat. It attracts dust in an extraordinary way, so try to keep your working area as clean as possible. Wash your brushes thoroughly after contact with varnish.

Wood filler

Fine-surface, ready-mixed filler is the best type to use on furniture. It has a tendency to shrink and sink further into the holes and cracks as it dries, so you may have to apply a second layer and let that dry before sanding it down to the smoothness of the surrounding surface. Store the can upside down.

Metal primer

This protects metal objects from rust by sealing them from air and water. For surfaces that are already rusty, you can use rust transformer, a special rust-removing primer.

Ready-painted metal does not require a primer, but can have the finish painted straight onto it. This also applies to plastic: either paint the finish directly or give the object a tinted semigloss undercoat first. Painting soft plastic is not recommended as it is liable to crack and may even react against the paint.

Sable brushes

Sable brushes are the finest brushes available, with fine, elegant tips for your most beautiful and detailed work. A couple of well-pointed sables, ranging in size between No. 4 and No. 7, will meet most requirements but try to use the size that is most appropriate for the job in hand. Beware of cheap soft-hair brushes, such as squirrel, which will only make your work more difficult.

Flat fitch brushes

These are good-quality brushes, springy and resilient, yet they do not scratch the paint. Buy hog-bristle brushes if you can, with bristles of about one inch in length. You will probably find that No. 8 and No. 10 are the most useful for undercoating and glazing small objects.

Decorator's brushes

These are black-bristled, heavy-duty brushes, which range in width from about ½ inch to 3 inches. You will need a selection of these for undercoating, glazing and varnishing larger objects.

Fan brushes

Use these for wood-graining. They have splayed bristles and, when pulled over a surface with a light hand, they leave grain marks in the wood.

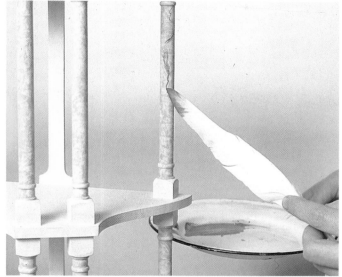

Feathers

Goose or turkey feathers are often sold for their quills but you will need to use their fine feather tips to apply veins to marble. Choose feathers with the sharpest tips.

Stencil brushes

These have compacted, stubby bristles and must be held at right angles to the stencil.

Badger softener brush

This is a large, soft, bushy brush. It magically transforms marbling when brushed very gently over the wet glaze, which more than compensates for its expense.

Sandpaper

This comes in various grades. You will need medium, fine and very fine. Try different grades to see which works best with each surface. There is no point in sanding bare wood; always raise the grain first with a quick, thin coat of flat white.

Containers and other equipment

You can use anything which is not made of thin plastic (which would be dissolved by the mineral spirits) for holding paint: old cans, for example, paper cups and glass jars. Mineral spirits containers are made of a special, heavy-duty plastic and, when empty, they can be cut across with a craft knife to create a receptacle.

Old pie plates are a good size and shape to use as a palette. If you clean your plate the same day with a rag and mineral spirits, the left-over paint should come off quite easily.

Glazes will survive for a few days if kept in a can or jar and well covered with plastic wrap. If you have to leave an uncompleted job for more than one or two days, mix up a double quantity of the glaze because the more you have, the better it will keep.

CARING FOR YOUR BRUSHES

If you keep your brushes in good condition, they will last a lot longer. I have old favorites who have been with me for years and I have used them every day. Do not leave brushes out to dry because they will go stiff and never recover.

If you have to leave your painting for a while, wrap the brush up in a rag that has been soaked in mineral spirits. When you finish working, keep it in a can of mineral spirits and then wash it as soon as possible.

Wipe off any paint that you can with a rag. Soak the brush in 2 to 3 inches of mineral spirits in an old can or paint bucket. Work the bristles of the brush energetically against the bottom of the can for a few minutes. Alternatively, you can scrub the paintbrush against a draining board. Be more delicate with sable brushes and don't bash them too hard. If the brush is still very dirty, use some fresh mineral spirits.

Wash the brush in detergent and warm water, once again working the liquid into the top of the bristles. Finally, rinse the brush in warm water, shake it and leave it on its side to dry.

Basic Techniques

THE first step of all, which is fundamental to almost all of the finishes in this book, is PREPARING AND UNDERCOATING the surface of the object, whether it is raw wood, already painted wood, metal or plastic. Once you have done this, you are likely to use a combination of three basic painting techniques: DRAGGING, RAGGING and VARNISHING. Most of the other techniques—for example, lacquering and distressing—are refinements of these.

All three are based on the application of a glaze: a thin coating of oil color mixed with mineral spirits and white paint. The aim is to allow the undercoat to glow through, giving life to the painted effect. Be careful, however, not to add too much white or the result will be a pasty and opaque glaze which will lie in ridges where you have applied it, instead of flowing thinly over the area. For decorative painting, such as lining out and bambooing, your glaze should be thicker with more white and more oil stainers in it to create a clear, strong impact.

PREPARING AND UNDERCOATING

For raw wood, follow steps 1–5 and then step 7. For ready-painted wood, follow steps 4–5 and then step 7. For bare metal, follow steps 6–7.

1. For undercoating raw wood, mix half to two thirds of flat white paint with half to one third of white spirit. The consistency of the mixture is important. It should soak into the wood and raise the rough, scratchy fibers of the grain. If the mixture is too thick, it will be hard to apply and will build up into heavy ridges. If it is too thin, it will drip and the paint will not cover the object thoroughly.

2. Using a fitch or decorator's brush, apply the paint to the surface lightly and evenly, following the grain of the wood. Make sure that you cover one area completely before beginning another. If you leave any wet edges to dry and then go back over them, you will end up with two overlapping coats of paint which will stand out as a ridge.

3. Leave the object for about 16 hours until it is thoroughly dry.

4. Rub the surface with sandpaper. Feel the surface as you go to avoid missing any areas. Wipe the surface with a rag and mineral spirits to remove the dust.

5. Fill any holes or cracks in the wood with fine-surface, ready-mixed wood filler. Leave to dry for a couple of hours before sanding it flush with the surface.

6. The first step in preparing metal for a painted finish is to apply a coat of metal primer.

7. With all types of surface, apply the semigloss undercoat as evenly as possible without any drips or rough brush marks. Two coats are adequate, although the first coat should be thinned down slightly with mineral spirits, which will help it to flow. Complete each coat in a single session unless you can stop neatly at a natural joint, such as the top of a chair leg. If you return to a half-finished surface after it has started to dry, the edge of the previous coat will not blend with the new coat and the result will be a rough, uneven area when the paint dries.

DRAGGING

As the photographs show, completely different effects can be created by applying one of three different techniques to the same basic color. The aim of dragging is to rearrange the paint once you have applied it to the surface so that it appears to run in a single direction. The mixture should be thicker than that used for ragging and should not be liable to drip. To achieve the consistency of very thin cream, you will need to use flat white paint (for body) and then add the pigments—in this case, crimson and cadmium scarlet. Add a little linseed oil to keep the mixture open, particularly if it is to be applied over a large surface. The only problem with flat white is that it lends a slightly bluish cast to the mixture, which you may need to counteract by adding yellow or raw sienna (from the opposite side of the color wheel).

Apply the paint thoroughly to one area of the surface at a time with a 1 inch or 2 inch decorator's brush. Then take a glazing brush and drag it through the glazed surface in straight, parallel lines up one stretch and down the next. Try to complete each stretch with one continuous stroke rather than with several back-and-forth strokes. The type of brush you use will affect the quality of the dragging. A flat glazing brush will leave firm lines and a strong impression. A soft, floppy decorator's brush with densely packed bristles, on the other hand, will leave a subtle impression of closely spaced lines. Hold the glazing brush at the ferrule.

DRAGGING is the basis for WOOD-GRAINING and DISTRESSING. With DISTRESSING, you allow the glaze, tinted with raw umber or black, to collect in the moldings in order to give an impression of wear and tear and age.

HANDY HINTS

The first coat of flat white is apt to splatter everywhere because the paint is so thin. Protect surrounding furniture and floors with old newspapers.

Remove paint from clothes by rubbing immediately with mineral spirits on a rag.

Keep the glaze for a day or two after use. If the paint on the object is smudged or chipped, you will be able to retouch it invisibly. Remixing the same color is extremely difficult.

When painting paneled objects, such as doors, check that drips of paint do not collect in the corners of the moldings and dribble down the edges of the panels. Simply wipe or brush them away before they dry.

Never use a plastic cup when mixing a glaze that contains mineral spirits; it will dissolve the plastic. Use a paper cup or a tin instead.

RAGGING

For ragging, the glaze should be slightly thinner than that used for dragging—more like the consistency of milk. Mix a glaze consisting, in this case, of a little flat white paint, crimson and cadmium scarlet, linseed oil and lots of mineral spirits. It does not matter if the mixture drips a bit. Make the mixture quite strong in color because, when you remove much of the paint with the rag, the effect will become much paler. Apply the glaze to a small area and rag it before you proceed—to check that the texture, weight and intensity of the color is as required once ragged.

Apply the glaze quickly but thoroughly to an entire surface of the object with a decorator's brush. Next, crumple a piece of rag in your hand and dab the glazed surface lightly, removing the paint as you go. The way you hold the rag will affect the type of surface you create. Experiment until you achieve a texture that you like.

If you want a very pale finish, keep rearranging the rag in your hand so that the pad in contact with the surface is clean. If you want a tightly patterned background, dab the surface with the same piece of rag, even though it may have become quite sodden with paint. If you want a cloudy effect, dab very softly. If you want a subtle, consistently mottled pattern, go over it again and again to create a texture that resembles the effects of stippling. Keep twisting the rag around in your hand so as not to create repetitive patterns; if, for example, the rag has a great diagonal crease down the middle, it will leave a repetitive print.

RAGGING is the basis for MARBLING and for LACQUERING. In the case of lacquering, you rag the surface of the object and then apply a coat of tinted varnish to soften the contrast with the tightly textured background.

HANDY HINTS

Glaze or drag one area of the surface at a time—before the paint has time to dry. For this reason, it is easier to drag pieces of furniture which divide naturally into self-contained surfaces, such as chair legs or table tops, than to drag whole walls.

Try not to leave telltale marks that betray where you have stopped and started. Continue right to the top or bottom of a stretch, therefore, instead of stopping halfway along. If you do have to brush back up a little at the edges to join and complete a downward stroke, lift your brush away gently at the join so as not to leave a mark.

Consult the color wheel on page 18. If you want to shift an existing color slightly, without transforming it, varnish it with a color from the opposite side of the wheel. Thus, if you want to make a blue greener, apply tinted yellow or green varnish. It's probably better to experiment first, however.

VARNISHING

Varnishing can fulfil two functions: it protects the painted finish and, if tinted, it can be used to modify or shift the original color of the surface. In this case, I added some crimson and cadmium scarlet to the eggshell varnish and then thinned the mixture with mineral spirits. (You cannot add more than about ½ inch squeeze of oil stainer to less than a quarter of a can of varnish or the mixture will become streaky.) Apply the varnish with a soft 2 inch decorator's brush (if the area is quite large) and then brush it out in all directions to achieve an even coverage. For extra control, hold the brush down by the ferrule.

VARNISHING is the basis for TORTOISESHELLING and for re-creating MALACHITE. The major difference is that, with tortoiseshelling, you apply more color onto the wet varnish as a second step. In addition, most of the techniques in the book involve varnishing as a final stage.

DRAGGING, RAGGING AND VARNISHING

These three basic techniques underlie all the processes in this book. Once you have mastered them, you can develop your own variations. You can combine them in new ways to achieve a blend of colors and textures, laying one on top of another: for example, by dragging a quick-drying tinted varnish to create a distressed, antique look. And you can add a host of new techniques to your repertory, such as spattering and applying paint with a fan brush.

HOW TO HOLD THE BRUSH

Brush control is the key to successful painting: the more you practice, the more comfortable you will feel with your brushes and the more you will develop favorites among them. When handling larger brushes, hold them close to the ferrule, which is the metal band keeping the bristles in place. This will give you maximum control and will also be less tiring. Make your brush work for you, pressing quite hard at first to cover the surface well with paint and then more lightly to smooth the paint out in a gliding movement. The final finish will depend on how firmly or gently you use your brush; again, it is a matter of trying different pressures until you are familiar with its possibilities.

Just because sables are such fine brushes does not mean that they should not work equally hard for you. In our Western culture, we have been taught from childhood to hold our pens and pencils at a 45-degree angle to the surface, resting the hand on the paper. Our natural inclination is to do the same with a sable brush. Try, instead, to imitate the Chinese, holding your sable at 90 degrees with your right hand above the surface and your little finger resting on the surface to steady your hand. Once you have overcome the initial strangeness of this technique, you will actually end up with far more control over the brush.

Creating Color

YOU do not need an art-school training to understand and work with color. Simply by memorizing a few basic rules, and trusting your instincts, the possibilities of color become endlessly fascinating. To this end, the purpose of all the recipes in this book is to provide some general guidelines which you can then adapt as much as you like.

The best way to judge a color you have mixed and applied is by standing well back and contemplating it. If you curl your index finger inside your thumb to create a hole about one inch across, you can isolate a color from those surrounding it. A color does not work in isolation but reacts with the colors around it to confuse your perception of the color in question.

Deciding which color to paint a piece of furniture is the first decision. You can either match the object to the color of the rest of the room or pick up one or two complementary colors. If you want to match the object to a specific color, it is always easier to use a snippet of fabric or paper as a guide instead of trying to paint from memory. Also, remember that colors darken as they dry. It is a good idea, therefore, to dry off a patch of paint before embarking on the whole painting project in order to check what the finished effect will be. When mixing complementary colors, there is quite a fine balance to be achieved. On the one hand, the contrast should not jar; on the other hand, if you are too cautious and the colors are too similar, they will not set the object off at all. Beware of effects, therefore, that rely solely on the subtle combination of neutral colors, such as beiges, creams and grays.

Most rooms can carry two contrasting colors: for example, pinks and greens or yellows and blues. Once you start introducing more than two colors rather than shades of the existing colors, the effect will begin to look fussy. For example, if the walls are yellow and the curtains have a yellow and blue pattern on a cream background, you could take the cream background as the basic color for your chairs with a decorative pattern that picks up the blue in the curtain print. If you had painted the chairs in the same yellow as the walls, they might have toned in so comprehensively as to lose any impact. If you then decide to wood-grain a bookcase in the same room, a pale, honey-colored wood, such as maple or walnut, might look splendid.

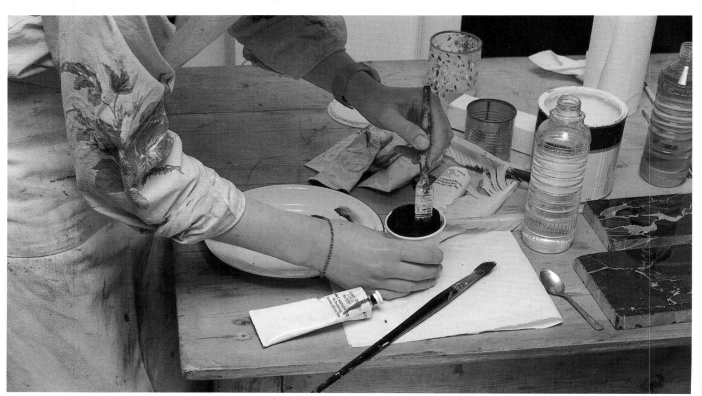

THE COLORS

The following colors form a basic selection from which you can mix any of the glazes in the book:

Primary Colors	Earth Colors
Lemon chrome	Raw umber
Cadmium scarlet	Burnt umber
Crimson	Raw sienna
Ultramarine	Burnt sienna
Viridian	

EARTH COLORS

These are comforting colors which give an instant feeling of age and authority to any piece of painted furniture. They are fundamental for wood-graining and marbling. It may seem surprising to include four browns in such a restricted palette— there is only one blue, for example—but they are all very different, either when used on their own or when mixed with a primary color. The two raw colors are paler and cooler versions of the two burnt earth colors.

Cadmium scarlet: An intensely bright red, cadmium scarlet is a pigment of medium strength. When mixed with lemon chrome, it gives a clear orange and, when mixed with raw sienna and white, a dusty peach. With crimson or burnt sienna, it will produce a rich, deep red.

Crimson: Despite its deep, luxurious, purple red and its association with pageantry, crimson is a weak pigment. Added to white and ultramarine, it gives a velvety mauve or purple. It is also useful for deepening and softening the impact of bright cadmium scarlet.

Ultramarine: A pure, rich blue, ultramarine is quite a weak pigment which is easily mixed with small amounts of green and yellow to create turquoise and with crimson, burnt umber and white to create a powdery Wedgwood blue. Ultramarine was once very expensive, which is why Renaissance artists used it so lavishly in the painting of the Virgin's robes: not only to honor her, but also to show off the wealth of the commissioning patron.

Viridian: A bright, bluish green, viridian is a pigment of medium strength which needs to be well stirred since it is not always very finely ground. It mixes well with lemon chrome to give a clear grassy green or with earth colors, such as raw sienna and raw umber, to achieve that old, gloomy green so beloved of English furniture painters. It also works well with ultramarine and black to create a clean, liquid turquoise.

Lemon chrome: An all-purpose yellow, lemon chrome is a very strong pigment which creates a cold effect. It mixes naturally with most colors except crimson. With black, it produces a very dark, acid green. With white, it counteracts the blueness of the base paint, creating a cool, greenish white.

Raw umber: The coolest of the earth colors, raw umber is a soft greenish brown which counteracts the brightness both of white and of the warm colors.

Burnt umber: A richer, chocolate-colored brown, burnt umber is the basis for dark woods. When mixed with black and a speck of white, it counteracts the blueness in the black and creates a warm brownish off-black.

Raw sienna: A golden, sandy brown, raw sienna is used in glazes for pale woods and yellow marbles. When mixed with white, it creates a rich cream color; it can also be used for toning down greens and pinks.

Burnt sienna: The richest, reddest and hottest of the earth colors, burnt sienna is used in coral and terracotta glazes. Because of the strength of the pigment, it mixes well only with warm primary colors.

BLACK

A fiercely strong pigment, black must be treated with respect and in small quantities. A dash of black can give authority to a glaze and it is extremely useful for adding sharp definition to the veins in marbles and stones or to the grain of mahogany. When mixed with scarlet, it creates a raw, foxy brown and, when mixed with lemon chrome, a strong and successful acid green.

WHITE

White is the joker in the pack in that I use it exclusively as a medium for other colors rather than as a color in its own right. Many of the techniques in this book are hundreds of years old and the aim of many of the finished effects is to make the objects look older than they are. In order to achieve this, we have to contend with white paint. Brilliant white, as it is known, is in fact a bluey white. It was invented this century and is often out of keeping with the age of both the traditional techniques and the objects themselves. You may need to counteract the blue in the paint by adding raw umber or raw sienna. This will take away some of its sheer brilliance and make it look softer and older.

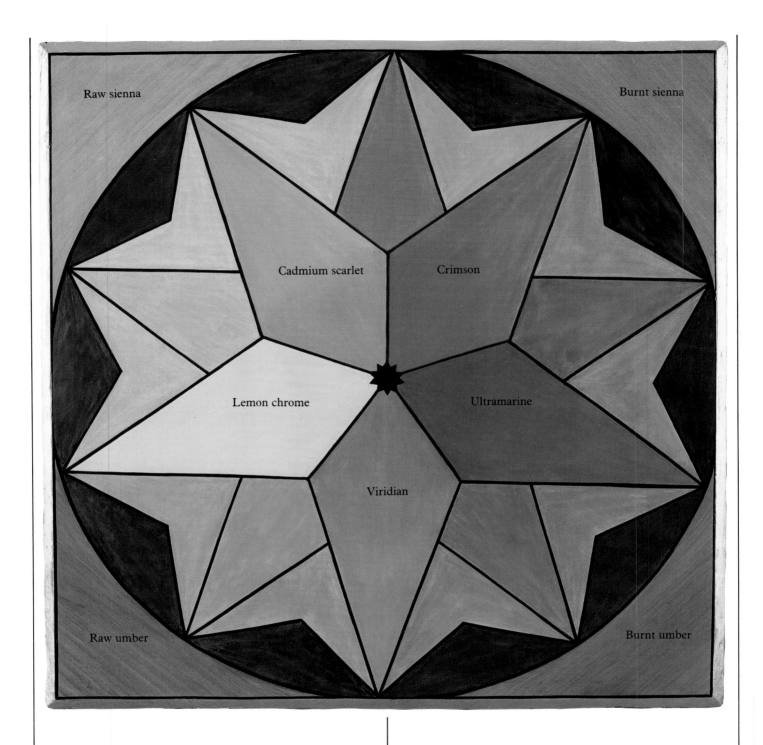

Raw sienna

Burnt sienna

Cadmium scarlet

Crimson

Lemon chrome

Ultramarine

Viridian

Raw umber

Burnt umber

Color Wheel

THINKING logically about color can unlock many of its mysteries. The five primary colors I use are linked in a spectrum toward the center of the color wheel. Although they are shown here in their purest and brightest forms, they can be diluted with white, deepened with black, mixed with other primary colors or toned down by the addition of an earth color. The color wheel illustrates the effect of mixing each of the colors with its neighbors. For example, when you mix lemon chrome with

viridian, the result will be the grass green that lies between them on the wheel. By adding white, raw umber and a little more lemon chrome to the grass green, you will achieve the softer, dirtier green that lies, in turn, between them. By adding black to lemon chrome plus a little viridian, you will achieve the very dark, acid green on the wheel. The color wheel also shows the opposite of each of the colors; for example, if you add a dash of ultramarine to a bright orange, the blue will take the heat out of the orange.

THE PROJECTS

THIS book does not claim to be a fully comprehensive manual of painting techniques. It is an introduction, rather, which takes more than 50 real projects to illustrate a variety of different techniques. You may, of course, not wish to paint marble panels on your car and you may have difficulty in buying a jardiniere on which to create a trompe l'oeil. This does not matter at all. The idea behind these projects is that you should be able to follow any one of the recipes and then apply it to whichever object is most appropriate to you.

Provided that you are interested in color and are reasonably patient, it is not difficult to achieve some measure of success. Practice is the key. If oil paints are a new medium for you, you cannot expect to master them in a morning's work. It is only gradually that you will begin to understand the properties of a glaze and to achieve a balance in color and consistency.

Here are some words of warning, however, before you begin. First, the quantities of paint suggested in these recipes may seem small; they were squeezed from tubes of a standard size and are the minimum amounts that you will require. Although glazes thinned with mineral spirits do go a long way, you will need to mix larger quantities if you are painting an object bigger than the one shown in that particular project. In any case, before you are completely confident, it may be a good idea to mix double quantities so that you can practice a little first and have some spare if you make a mistake. At all costs, avoid running out of glaze halfway through a project; it is extremely difficult to mix exactly the same color again.

Secondly, the strength of the pigments in the paint can vary. Although these recipes have been tested on well-known brands, different brands and even different batches can vary in intensity of color.

Thirdly, the times given for accomplishing a particular project are those that might be expected from someone who is fairly competent. They do not allow any scope for practicing or for wiping away mistakes; if you are less experienced, therefore, give yourself some extra time.

Above all, I wrote this book in the hope that it would be *used*. There is no need to follow the recipes too slavishly. Please adapt the techniques to different objects and alter the colors to suit your own surroundings.

DECORATIVE PAINTING

THIS chapter deals with some of the most obviously "painted" effects in painted furniture. The aim of most decorative painting is to create a trompe l'oeil: to deceive the eye into thinking that a two-dimensional surface has three dimensions by painting pretend moldings or by creating imaginary features in relief. The style, which relies on the way in which the sun strikes an object creating shadows and highlights, has been practiced for many years. Unlike many of the techniques in this book which are limited by their very nature—there are only so many woods or marbles, for example—decorative painting is open to a range of interpretations.

Broadly speaking, you should try to enhance the best features of a piece of furniture without actually disguising the material from

which it was made originally, although you might like to age it a little or adapt it to the existing color scheme of the room.

The first step is to apply a coat of glaze. It is then your skill with the brush and your choice of colors which will determine the effectiveness of the decoration. Your hand should be steady, yet confident. Practice is always rewarded because the finished effect should appear effortless. A flicker of shadow or a flash of highlight should look just like that, completed in one stroke rather than in a series of wobbly and hesitant little attempts.

Once you have mastered the technique, however, it is probably one of the most enjoyable to accomplish. You can create remarkably decorative patterns very quickly.

Materials (from left to right)
- Oil colors
- Flat white paint to give the glaze body
- Mineral spirits to thin the glaze
- Linseed oil
- Varnish to protect the object after decorating

Tools (from left to right)
- Cotton rag
- Scissors for cutting the tracing paper
- Masking tape for attaching the tracing paper

- A couple of fitch brushes (an old one with which to mix the paint and a new one for applying it)
- Plate on which to break down and mix the pigments
- A collection of sable brushes. At the back of the plate, a No. 5, a No. 7 and a No. 4; at the front, a ½ in.-wide flat sable brush.
- A paper cup and a can for mixing the paint
- Tracing paper for transferring the design onto the object
- Pencil (an HB for tracing the design onto the paper and a 2H for transferring the tracing onto the object)
- A couple of rulers
- Eraser

Standard Lamp with Painted Moldings

Time: ¾ hour for picking out.

Sources and applications: The picking out of molded features can add a touch of elegance to the most everyday object. The technique looks particularly effective on any piece of furniture that has moldings: cupboard doors, for example, picture-frames, chairs, standard lamps, doors and tables with molded legs.

Getting ready: Prepare the surface of the object. If it has been painted before, rub the surface down with sandpaper and wipe with a rag dampened with mineral spirits. Then, apply one or two coats of white semigloss (depending on the strength of the original color) and leave to dry. Mix a creamy, off-white glaze, consisting of flat white paint, raw sienna and a tiny speck of black, thinned down with mineral spirits and a drop of linseed oil. Apply a coat of this glaze thinly and evenly all over the lamp base in the direction of the wood.

STEP-BY-STEP RECIPE

1. Mix a glaze, consisting of:
- 1 teaspoon of flat white
- ¼ in. squeeze of lemon chrome
- ¼ in. squeeze of raw umber
- ¼ in. squeeze of viridian
- ¼ in. squeeze of raw sienna

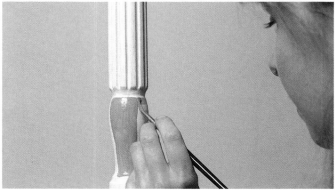

2. Take a No. 6 sable brush and apply the green glaze to all the existing convex moldings.

3. Leave to dry overnight and apply a coat of eggshell varnish.

HANDY HINTS

The joy of picking out is that you are simply selecting and emphasizing moldings that already exist; you don't have to invent shadows and highlights or trompe l'oeil. In order not to end up with an object striped like a zebra, decide first which moldings to pick out—in this case, I chose to pick out only the convex moldings. But, on another object, you could equally well decide to pick out just the concave moldings.

Keep it simple. If in doubt, leave more moldings plain than picked out.

Make sure that the edges are sharply painted.

Painted Easter Baskets

Time: About 1 hour per basket.

Sources and applications: Raw wicker or cane can look very cheap, but painted decoration transforms it immediately. Decorated baskets look particularly good in bedrooms, bathrooms and kichens, holding flowers, soaps or pot-pourri. Paint them in colors that pick up the color scheme of the room—to match the curtains, for example, or the wallpaper. In the case of the yellow-and-black basket, I picked up the yellow of the inset bathroom panels (see page 71). Alternatively, you could paint your baskets red-and-white or blue-and-white to pick up the colors of any check tablecloths you might have. The same technique is equally applicable to wicker waste-paper bins and laundry baskets. You can even create tartan patterns successfully if the wicker has a crisscross weave.

Getting ready: Undercoat the baskets with flat white paint and apply two coats of tinted semigloss.
- For the GREEN BASKET, tint white semigloss with raw umber to soften the sheer brilliance of the white.
- For the PINK BASKET, tint white semigloss a soft pale pink with cadmium scarlet and raw sienna.
- For the YELLOW BASKET, tint white semigloss with lemon chrome, raw sienna and cadmium scarlet.

STEP-BY-STEP RECIPE

1. For the GREEN BASKET, add viridian, lemon chrome and a drop of black and raw sienna to some white semigloss. Using the weave of the wicker as a guide, paint stripes on the basket with a No. 5 sable brush. The effect will look smarter and more solid if each of your stripes consists of both the prominent strips of wicker and the strips behind them.

2. For the PINK BASKET, mix a deep Burgundy red by adding crimson and a little black to the pale pink semigloss undercoat. Pick out bands at the bottom and toward the top of the basket. Make the stripes horizontal and about half an inch wide. To emphasize the twisted weave on the top rim and the handle, paint every other twist of the weave.

basket (in this case, fifteen) and divide this by the height of each square (say, five) to give you the number of squares (three) running up the basket. Then, make each square measure five strips of cane across. Paint the squares with a No. 6 sable brush, using either black semigloss paint or white semigloss stained black.

3. For the YELLOW BASKET, devise a checkered pattern by using the weave of the cane or wicker to divide the basket into squares. Count the number of strips of cane running horizontally across the

HANDY HINTS

Devise any number of patterns to decorate the baskets, using the weave of the wicker as your guide: diagonal stripes, diamonds, chevrons and stars, for example.

To add a final flourish—especially if you intend giving it as a present or filling it with Easter eggs, scent or soap—line the inside of the basket with fabric.

Trompe l'Oeil Jardiniere

Time: 3 hours for decorating, spread over 4 days; ½ hour for varnishing on the following day.

Getting ready: Apply an undercoat of white semigloss to the jardiniere and leave to dry.

STEP-BY-STEP RECIPE

1. Mix a pale blue glaze, consisting of:
- 2 teaspoons of flat white
- ½ in. squeeze of ultramarine
- ¼ in. squeeze of raw sienna
- ¼ in. squeeze of raw umber
- ½ teaspoon of linseed oil
- 2 teaspoons of mineral spirits to thin the glaze to a milky consistency

2. Test the color and consistency of the glaze on the object. Once you have applied the glaze, you should be able to draw your brush back through it quite easily. On the other hand, it should not be so thin as to drip.

3. Cover each surface of the jardiniere with as little glaze as you can. Then, without reloading your brush, draw it back through the glaze straight in the direction of the grain. The undercoat will show through and give the glaze a clean, light, soft finish. Leave the jardiniere to dry overnight. Keep the glaze in a cup covered with plastic wrap.

4. If you are nervous about making mistakes in the following steps, apply a coat of eggshell varnish in order to protect the glaze and leave to dry.

5. Cut a piece of tracing paper to fit the panel of the jardiniere. With an HB pencil, draw a square ½ inch in from the sides of the panel.

Draw a second square a further ½ inch in all round. Scallop out the corners of the two squares using a coin or a circular can lid.

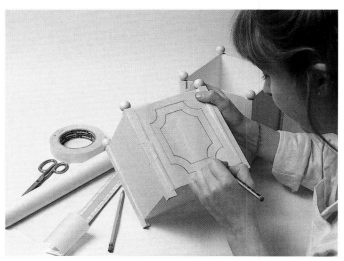

6. Turn the piece of tracing paper over and attach it to the panel with masking tape. Take a 2H pencil, which is slightly harder and sharper, and transfer the image of the square onto the panel. Repeat this process on each side of the jardiniere.

7. To make the original mixture (see step 1) a tone or two darker, add a little ultramarine and raw sienna.

8. Dip a flat ½-inch sable brush or a No. 7 sable brush into the new mixture and apply the glaze smoothly and evenly to each of the inset panels in turn. Take care to work within the pencil lines and try to keep the paint flowing so as not to leave any wet edges to dry. If possible, miter the corners for extra effect. Complete all the inset panels before commencing the columns; otherwise you are likely to smudge them with your hand. Paint the columns up the sides to match and leave to dry overnight.

9. Apply a coat of eggshell varnish and leave to dry for half a day. It will now be time to apply the shadow and highlight lines to create the illusion that the panels with scalloped corners are recessed.

10. Apply the highlight lines first. Dip a No. 4 sable brush with a good point into some flat white paint mixed with a little mineral spirits. The mixture should be thin enough to flow easily yet thick enough to read over the darker blue underneath. Imagine that the sun is coming from the top left-hand corner, creating shadows and highlights at the recessed edges, or returns, of the inset panel. The outer returns at the top and at the left will face away from the sun and will therefore cast shadows; the inner returns at the top and at the left will face the sun and will therefore be highlighted. Conversely, the outer returns at the bottom and at the right will face the sun and will be highlighted and the inner returns at the bottom and at the right will cast shadows. If all this seems rather complicated, look at a door with real panels to work out where the shadows and highlights fall.

Once you have decided, paint straight lines about ⅛ inch wide, keeping the corners as sharp as possible.

11. Next, apply the shadows. Add a hint of black, some ultramarine and some raw sienna to the darker mixture (step 7) to create a grayish blue shadow line. Apply with a No. 4 sable brush to the returns that you did not highlight. Make sure that you miter the corners. The jardiniere will suddenly take on a third dimension. Using the same mixture, paint the balls on top of each corner column and leave to dry.

12. Apply one or two coats of white semigloss, tinted a dark blue with raw sienna, ultramarine, black and viridian, to the insides of the jardiniere and apply a coat of eggshell varnish to the outside.

Miniature Chest of Drawers Decorated in Red and Gold

Time: 3 hours spread over 3 days; 15 minutes for varnishing on the following day.

Sources and applications: Simple classical patterns such as this work equally well on grand and on homely pieces of furniture. They look good on chests of drawers, running up and down chair legs and along the backs of chairs.

Getting ready: Apply an undercoat consisting of two thirds of flat white to one third of mineral spirits. Leave to dry for about 16 hours. Sand down to a smooth finish with medium-fine sandpaper. Then undercoat again with two coats of white semigloss tinted a rather lurid tangerine pink with burnt sienna, raw sienna and cadmium scarlet. Leave to dry overnight after each coat.

STEP-BY-STEP RECIPE

1. Mix a rich, Chinese red glaze, consisting of:
- 1 teaspoon of eggshell varnish (this glaze is based on varnish rather than on flat white paint to give it body and to create a bright, translucent finish)
- ⅜ in. squeeze of crimson
- ¼ in. squeeze of cadmium scarlet
- ¼ in. squeeze of burnt sienna
- a dash of burnt umber
- mineral spirits to dilute the glaze to the consistency of cream

2. Apply the glaze thinly and evenly to a single surface with a No. 10 fitch brush. Without reloading the brush, pull it back through the glaze in the direction of the grain so that the undercoat glows through the light, translucent coat of glaze. Repeat this process on each of the remaining surfaces in turn. Leave to dry overnight. The varnish in the mixture will speed up the drying process and leave you with a good, tough finish.

3. Cut a piece of tracing paper to fit half of the length of a drawer. Then fold the paper in half horizontally to find the halfway line. Divide it lengthwise into five equal sections and draw a pair of leaves in each section with an HB pencil—one of the leaves in each pair either side of the halfway line.　•

Make the leaves at the edge of the drawer progressively smaller than those at the center—to create an effect that tapers away toward the edge. Add a few little berries around the leaves. The point of using tracing paper in this instance is to ensure that the pattern repeats regularly and evenly.

4. Turn the tracing paper over and secure it to one half of a drawer with masking tape. Transfer the image onto the drawer by outlining the pattern clearly with a 2H pencil, pressing quite firmly. Try to outline the leaves in one smooth stroke of the pencil. Next, transfer the image to the same half of the other drawers. Turn the paper over and secure it to the other half of each of the drawers and repeat the process.

5. Mix a soft golden yellow glaze, consisting of a little flat white with raw sienna, burnt sienna and raw umber. Don't be worried if the color appears to be a rather grubby khaki on the plate, rather than a bright golden yellow. It will seem much brighter when you test it on the dark red background—and certainly more sympathetic than if you had used lemon chrome.

6. Test the color on the object and, when you are satisfied, apply the glaze to the pattern with a sable brush—either a No. 4 or a No. 6 or both. It is best to use as large a brush as you feel comfortable with in order to minimize the number of brush strokes. Begin with the stem, which runs horizontally across the middle of the drawer, and then paint the leaves on either side. Try to complete each leaf in two brush strokes—one on either side of the central vein. Begin at the base of the leaf and paint in the direction of natural growth, lifting your brush abruptly at the tip of the leaf to leave a sharp point. There is no need to follow the tracing slavishly; you are trying to create an impression as simply and as economically as possible rather than executing a brilliant still-life.

7. Using a coin, about 1 inch in diameter, pencil quarter-circles facing inward on each corner of the top of the chest. These will form the scalloped corners of an inset panel. Pencil a line all round the top of the chest, about ⅜ inch in from the edges, to connect the scalloped corners.

8. Dip a No. 4 sable brush into your paint mixture (step 5) and apply a thin border—about ⅛ inch wide—over the pencil lines. Start in one corner and follow the line smoothly all the way round, turning the box when necessary. Hold your third and fourth fingers straight and stiff to act as a guide and steady your hand by gripping the outside edge of the chest.
Leave to dry overnight.

9. Apply the shadow and highlight lines to emphasize the shapes of the leaves. Do the shadows first because there will be more of these and the placing of them will determine where you put the highlights. For the shadow lines, mix a dark brown glaze on a plate, consisting of:
- a brushtipful of raw umber
- a brushtipful of raw sienna
- a brushtipful of black
- a drop of mineral spirits to make the mixture flow

10. Apply the shadow mixture with a finely pointed No. 4 or No. 5 sable brush. Give each leaf a dark spine—beginning at the base of the leaf and, in one continuous stroke, lifting your brush away toward the end to leave a tapering tip. Add a shadow at the bottom of each berry and a shadow beneath the horizontal stem. Also, paint a shadow below and behind each leaf—the sun, as always, is shining from above. Take comfort and confidence from the fact that this is a very small, simple and stylized pattern; you don't need to be precise. The more you worry, the worse it will look.

11. For the flecks of highlight, mix a little flat white on a plate with some raw sienna and a few brushtipfuls of mineral spirits. Don't worry if the color looks quite dark—almost a creamy beige—on the plate. It will read as white against the background.

12. Apply the highlights with the same sable brush (remembering to clean it first) but make them slightly thinner than the shadows. Place them on the other side of the foliage from the shadows—that is, around the top of each leaf, as a tiny semicircle of light on the top of each berry, and above the horizontal stem. There is no highlight running along the spine of each leaf. Work in the opposite direction to that in which you applied the shadows. Since the light is coming from above, the highlight should be biggest and brightest at the top of the leaf, tapering to a fine point around the base. When applying either shadows or highlights, extend the leaf by painting over the red rather than over the golden yellow.

13. Leave to dry overnight and then apply a coat of eggshell varnish.

Dragged Kitchen Cupboards

Time: ½ hour per cupboard.

Sources and applications: This effect, created by dragging and then by picking out, suits cupboards, doors, chests of drawers and window shutters, particularly in kitchens, bathrooms and bedrooms.

Getting ready: If the existing finish is raw wood, apply a coat of flat white paint and rub down with sandpaper. Once it has been undercoated in this way, apply two coats of white semigloss.

STEP-BY-STEP RECIPE

1. In a paint bucket, mix a glaze consisting of:
- ¾ in. of flat white poured into the bucket
- 1¾ in. squeeze of ultramarine
- ½ in. squeeze of raw umber
- ¼ in. squeeze of burnt umber
- mineral spirits to thin the glaze to the consistency of cream
- 2 tablespoons of linseed oil
  (These quantities are sufficient for about six cupboards.)

2. Apply the glaze with a 2 in. decorator's brush to one section of the cupboard at a time. Do the central panel of one of the doors first (1). As soon as you have covered this area—and therefore before the paint has begun to dry—take a thin glazing brush and drag it smoothly back through the glaze so that the white eggshell undercoat shows through. Next, take a No. 10 fitch brush and repeat the same process, glazing and dragging the other areas in the following order: along the internal rails (2); up and down the internal stiles (3); along the external rails; and finally, up and down the external stiles (4). If necessary, remove the knobs and drag these separately. Note that this order is exactly that which you would use when dragging any type of door.

3. Glaze and drag the frame of each of the cupboards with the fitch. Do the horizontal sides first and then the vertical sides.

4. Leave the cupboards to dry. This will take a day because the oil retards the drying process.

5. Mix a rich dark-blue glaze, consisting of:
- 2 tablespoons of the original glaze (step 1)
- 1 in. squeeze of ultramarine
- ¼ in. squeeze of raw umber
- ¼ in. squeeze of black

6. Apply the glaze smoothly with a No. 5 or a No. 6 sable brush to the edges of the inset panels. Try to paint each edge with no more than two brush strokes so that there are no stop-and-start marks. The aim of these shadowy lines is to catch your eye as you walk past the cupboards; they should create an impression, so keep them strong and simple. Leave to dry overnight.

7. Apply a coat of eggshell varnish.

HANDY HINTS

The purpose of dragging is to emphasize the grain of the "wood", even if the original surface is plastic.

The arrangement of bristles on the brush determines the effect you will achieve. If you want a marked effect, use a brush with fewer bristles. If you want a softer, more subtle grain, use a soft decorator's brush with densely packed bristles.

The original glaze becomes hard to drag after about five minutes. If you do not divide the object into self-contained sections, the paint will have dried before you begin to drag.

Wipe away any mistakes with a rag and mineral spirits.

When dragging, make sure that the brush is free from paint. You should not be applying paint at this stage; the aim is to rearrange it.

Don't forget to drag the returns on the tops of the drawers and on the insides of the cupboard doors. Then check that the paint has not crept back round to the front and, if it has, just drag the brush lightly back through it.

Faux Wedgwood Lamp Base

Time: 1½ hours.

Sources and applications: Ribbons, bows and garlands form a traditional pattern often seen on painted furniture. I traced this one from the arm and leg of a chair and then painted it onto the blue background in a soft white to create the illusion of Wedgwood ware.

Getting ready: Apply a coat of flat white paint.

STEP-BY-STEP RECIPE

1. To achieve a Wedgwood blue, mix in a cup:
- 2 tablespoons of flat white
- ½ in. squeeze of ultramarine
- a flash of crimson

2. Test the color on an area of the surface; it should be a powdery, almost purple blue. When you are satisfied, apply the paint with either a small decorator's brush (a ¾ inch or 1 inch) or a No. 10 fitch brush. Coat the object as thickly and evenly as you dare. Leave to dry overnight.

3. Make a tracing of the garland with an HB pencil. Measure the circumference of the lamp base with a tape measure and divide it into five sections. Turn the paper over, attach it and transfer the image with a 2H pencil to create five equally spaced garlands.

4. In a cup, mix a speck of raw umber with some flat white paint. Apply this to the pattern with a No. 4 sable brush. Begin at the bow, move down the stem and then paint each leaf at the end of a little stalk. Do each half of the leaf separately. The first half of the leaf is a continuation of the stalk. Then, begin the second half at the base of the leaf, lifting the brush gently away toward the tip to leave a fine point.

Paint the swags of ribbon between the garlands. Try to leave the impressions of the brush strokes because it is these that make the ribbon appear to lie in folds. Continue the pattern around the lamp base.

Develop the pattern as you like. You might paint stylized lotus leaves—with their tips about ¾ inch apart—toward the top and bottom of the lamp base. This time, begin at the tip and apply greater pressure on the brush as you move down toward the base—completing each leaf in about three brush strokes. In addition, you might pick out the pedestal with a rope pattern, made out of interlocking S's and comprising one brush stroke per strand. Finally, you might paint little circles around the rim at the top of the lamp base to create the illusion of beading.

Flower-Painted Hot Water Can

Time: 3½ hours for applying the glaze and painting the flowers, spread over 2 days.

Sources and applications: Painted flowers, such as this jasmine, look good climbing up a chair leg or around a lamp base, encircling a little box or entwined around window blinds.

Getting ready: Scrub away the rust with a wire brush. Be quite firm and energetic. Using an old brush, apply rust transformer to the rusty parts of the metal only. Rust transformer converts the rust into an inactive black compound which resists further rusting. You can actually see the reaction taking place as the rust transformer dries, changing from a milky white to black. Leave the object to dry overnight.

Mix an undercoat, consisting of white semigloss, tinted a lurid pink with crimson and cadmium scarlet. Apply one or two coats of this mixture with a No. 10 fitch brush.

STEP-BY-STEP RECIPE

1. In a cup, mix a dark red glaze, consisting of:
- 1 teaspoon of the original pink undercoat
- 2 teaspoons of eggshell varnish
- 1 in. squeeze of crimson (you need so much because red is a weak pigment)
- ½ in. squeeze of cadmium scarlet
- ⅛ in. squeeze of black
- mineral spirits to thin the glaze to a creamy consistency

2. Apply the glaze thinly and evenly with a No. 10 fitch brush so that the undercoat shows through a little. Without reloading the brush, drag it up and down back through the glaze to rearrange the paint. The marks of the bristles will leave an impression of age and decrepitude. Leave to dry overnight.

3. Decide on a design for the decoration. In this case, inspiration came from a little jasmine plant I had in the house. The simplicity of the plant and the fact that there are only two colors—white for the flowers and green for the leaves—makes this an ideal choice for freehand decoration. In addition, the tendrils of the plant will twine around the handle and the spout. Take a pencil and draw the basic pattern of the stalk and the leaves onto the can; make a tracing first if this will give you greater confidence.

4. On a plate, mix a dark green glaze that will stand out against the crimson background, consisting of:
- ¼ in. squeeze of lemon chrome
- ¼ in. squeeze of viridian
- ¼ in. squeeze of raw sienna
- ⅛ in. squeeze of black
- a brushtipful of flat white for extra body
- mineral spirits to make the mixture flow easily

6. On a plate, mix a glaze for the flowers, consisting of:
- a little flat white
- a drop of the green glaze (step 4)
- a dash of lemon chrome

5. Paint the stem and the leaves onto the can with a No. 4 or a No. 5 sable brush. Note that both the leaves and the flowers branch off the stem in pairs—one leaf at the end of its little stalk on either side of the stem. Paint half of each leaf at a time, beginning at the base and lifting the brush away towards the tip to leave a fine point. Then do the other half. At the same time, apply the stalks for the flowers—these range from about ½ inch to 2 inches in length. It will help if you hold the brush at right angles to the surface, using your little finger as a support for greater control.

7. Apply the flowers with a No. 4 sable brush. Vary their sizes so that some are little more than long, sharply pointed buds and others are full-blown flowers with six petals and a stamen in the center. As with the leaves, begin each petal at the base.

Black Lacquer Dining Table

Time: 4½ hours spread over 3 days, plus 1 hour for varnishing on the following day.

Sources and applications: The black lacquer look suits large surfaces, such as chests of drawers, cupboards and boxes. Take the oriental atmosphere a little further by adding yellow lines that are reminiscent of a chinoiserie motif.

Getting ready: In this case, the existing finish was an ugly dark brown varnish. Therefore, it was enough to rub the surface with fine-grain sandpaper and then wipe it clean with a rag and white spirit. If the existing finish had been a different color, however, or if the grain had been very prominent, it would also have needed a coat of semigloss, tinted a rich chestnut brown.

STEP-BY-STEP RECIPE

1. In a tin, mix a glaze, consisting of:
- 1 tablespoon of flat black paint or black semigloss
- 1½ in. squeeze of cadmium scarlet
- ½ teaspoon of linseed oil
- a brushtipful of flat white
- mineral spirits to thin the glaze to a creamy consistency

2. Apply the paint evenly with a 1 inch decorator's brush to one surface of the table at a time—a leg, for example, the base frame, or a section of the table top. For these purposes, I divided this large table top into thirds.

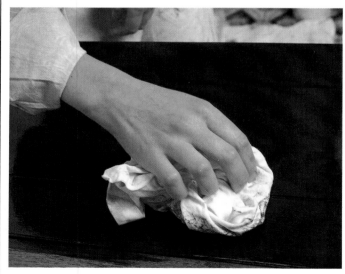

3. Once you have applied the glaze, take a rag and fold it into a soft, flat, smooth pad. Blot the surface quite gently to create a subtle, mottled, closely textured background and leave to dry overnight. If it appears that you are removing a lot of paint, leave the glazed surface for a few minutes before continuing so that the paint has time to dry a little.

4. To a tin half full of varnish, add about ½ inch squeeze of crimson and ¼ inch squeeze of black to create a browny, purply black. Apply the tinted varnish with a 1 inch or 1½ inch decorator's brush and leave to dry in a dust-free atmosphere.

5. For the decoration, mix a yellow glaze, consisting of:
- 2 tablespoons of white semigloss
- 1½ in. squeeze of raw sienna
- 1½ in. squeeze of lemon chrome
- ¼ in. squeeze of burnt sienna
- mineral spirits to make the paint flow from the brush (but not so much that the glaze will not read against the dark background.

6. With a No. 4 or a No. 5 sable brush, pick out yellow lines about ⅛ inch wide to separate the panels in the table top. Position your ruler about ½ inch from the line to be painted and use it as a guide, resting your middle finger, third finger and little finger on the ruler and pulling the brush along in as continuous a line as possible with your thumb and index finger. You will then have to go back over and strengthen the lines you have painted. Add crisscross squares at the edges to simulate a basic form of trellis-work. In this case, the fact that the table was composed of leaves and the panels already existed made the task easier. However, if your table does not have panels already, mark a border about 3 inches in from the edge with a pencil and ruler. Then divide the top of the table crossways into equal rectangular panels. Wipe away any mistakes with a piece of kitchen paper or, if the paint has begun to dry, with a rag and mineral spirits.

7. Pick out the four edges of each of the legs in exactly the same way—either using any existing moldings or creating new lines about ⅛ inch wide. Leave to dry overnight.

8. Apply a thick coat of clear semigloss or gloss varnish.

HANDY HINTS

When decorating table tops, keep the design simple. The more complicated the design, the more likely it is to clash with the objects you place on top of it.

Lining out is tricky, but don't worry; your technique will improve with practice.

When ragging each section of the table top, leave a little bit at the edge unragged. Once you have applied the glaze to the adjoining section, rag the area of the first section which you had left unragged and then proceed to rag all but the very edge of the second section. This technique of glazing and ragging overlapping sections ensures that there are no telltale cross-over marks.

It is better not to assume that the edge of the table is a straight line; use a ruler, instead, as a guide for lining out.

Reviving a Bedside Table

Time: 1½ hours for decorating.

Sources and applications: I copied this simple classical motif from a piece of 18th-century painted furniture which I had photographed. Patterns such as this are easy and economical. By turning a series of circles into two sets of interlocking waves, you can achieve an interesting and old-fashioned effect for the minimum of effort. Similar motifs would look good on kitchen cupboards, around the edges of a bath, along the borders of a bedroom or all around a circular table top.

Getting ready: Wash the table with a rag dipped in mineral spirits to remove the grease. When re-creating color to match old painted furniture, you have to feel your way gradually. For this battered old bedside table, I mixed a little flat white with tiny squeezes of lemon chrome, raw sienna, viridian, ultramarine and black, plus a few drops of eggshell varnish to help the paint cling.

Using a No. 5 sable brush, test the color on the object. Remember that the color will darken as the paint dries; indeed, many pieces of old furniture are characterized by great dark blobs which betray the fact that they have been retouched. If the color is correct when wet, it will be too dark when dry. Therefore, to check that the color matches, dry a small area of paint with a hair dryer for about 10 seconds. The color will change before your eyes from light, shiny and wet to dark, flat and matt.

When you are satisfied with the color, continue to retouch the object. Fill in just the hole that is damaged and don't paint over the edges of the crack, especially if the object is valuable. The aim is to retain as much of the original paint as possible. Bear in mind that some areas of the table may be darker than those which have been bleached by the sun over the years; so vary the color as you go.

STEP-BY-STEP RECIPE

1. Cut a piece of tracing paper to fit half of the length of a drawer. Measure it up into three sections—there will be 6 repeat patterns along the full length of the drawer—but bear in mind where the knobs will be so that the pattern does not go over them. Fold the paper in two horizontally to find the halfway line. Then, with an HB pencil, draw three contiguous circles which are centered along the halfway line. Turn the tracing paper over and attach it to half of the top drawer. Take a 2H pencil and transfer the circles onto the drawer. Repeat this process on all the other drawers, half by half.

2. Mix a mushroom-colored glaze consisting of:
- 1 tablespoon of white semigloss (rather than flat white because the glaze must be quite thick and opaque in order to show up against the dark background)
- ¼ in. squeeze of raw sienna
- ¼ in. squeeze of raw umber
- a speck of black
- a little mineral spirits to make the glaze flow

3. Apply the mixture with a No. 4 sable brush to the penciled lines. When painting circles, you will find it easier if you draw the brush toward yourself. Although we have all been taught to write and draw with the side of the hand resting on the surface, this technique restricts freedom of movement. It is better, in this case, to keep the brush as upright as possible, using your hand like a drawing compass, pivoted about the little finger. Keep the mixture thin enough to flow well, adding a little mineral spirits when necessary, but thick enough so that it shows up against the dark background.

4. Imagine that the circles form two sets of interlocking waves and that the waves beginning at the bottom left are those formed by a ribbon—thicker where the ribbon is viewed in its full width and thinner where it folds in on itself and is viewed sideways on. Apply some more paint with the sable brush, increasing the pressure in order to flatten the bristles and widen the wave where the ribbon is viewed in its full width and lifting the brush to its tip to emphasize the narrow lines where the ribbon is viewed sideways on. Be as economical as possible with your brush strokes.

6. Again using the same glaze and the same brush, apply the leaves to the stalks. Paint each leaf with two strokes—one either side of the central vein—varying the size of each leaf and its direction slightly.

7. Repeat the same process on the second drawer. But this time, reverse the pattern so that the waves of the ribbon begin at the top left and the waves comprising the stalk begin at the bottom left.

8. Finally, using a No. 4 or a No. 6 sable brush, paint a line about ⅜ inch wide all round the top of the chest to create an inset panel about 1 inch in from the edge. Leave to dry overnight.

5. Imagine that the series of waves beginning at the top left are those formed by the stem. Using the same glaze and the same brush, paint short stalks either side of the stem—perhaps four pairs of stalks per semicircle. As always, paint in the direction of natural growth—beginning with a slightly wider line at the base of each stalk, where it joins the stem, and lifting your brush away toward the end of the stalk to leave a fine point. Make sure that the stalks all face in the same direction.

Chair Decorated in a Classical Style

Time: 1½ hours.

Getting ready: Old furniture is often painted green but, in this case, I applied a pale blue glaze, consisting of flat white paint, ultramarine, raw sienna and black over an undercoat of white semigloss.

STEP-BY-STEP RECIPE

1. Using an HB pencil, draw an urn with swags, ribbons and bows onto a piece of tracing paper to fit the back of a chair. I copied this design from an old piece of painted furniture.

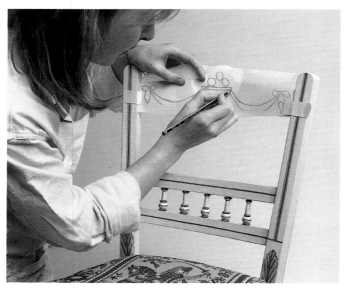

2. Turn the paper over and attach it to the chair with masking tape. With a 2H pencil, transfer the image onto the chair. Make the pencil lines flow evenly.

3. Mix a grayish blue, consisting of:
- 1 teaspoon of flat white
- ¾ in. squeeze of ultramarine
- ¼ in. squeeze of raw sienna
- a dash of crimson
- a dash of black
- mineral spirits to make it flow

4. Take a No. 6 sable brush and, brushing toward yourself with as few strokes as possible, block in the area between the pencil lines. Hold the brush at right angles to the surface for extra control and use your little finger to steady your hand. Use the tip of the brush to create fine points and apply a little pressure to flatten the brush when applying the thicker lines of the ribbon. Paint quickly to achieve an effortless effect. Leave the chair to dry for 3–4 hours.

5. Pour some of the original mixture (see step 3) onto a plate and add a little extra ultramarine and black to create a darker blue. To add an extra form and dimension to the motif and to sharpen the overall effect, quickly apply shadows to the background with a No. 4 sable brush. Search for inspiration in real life; look at the way creases, folds or relief cast shadows in cloth, on flowers or on pots. Sunlight shines from above. So make sure that the shadows are below rather than above each painted feature and leave a larger area unshadowed. Don't overdo it.

6. Decorate the rest of the chair, using the same color, and leave to dry. Finally, apply a coat of eggshell varnish.

Decorated Marble Shelf

Time: 3 hours spread over 3 days.

Getting ready: Apply a thin coat of flat white paint to the raw wood and leave to dry. Rub down with medium-fine sandpaper, apply two coats of white semigloss and leave to dry. Finally, rub the surface with very fine sandpaper and wipe with a rag and a little mineral spirits. This will remove any particles of dust that have stuck into the paint and should leave the surface smooth.

STEP-BY-STEP RECIPE

1. Mix a soft coral-pink glaze, consisting of:
- 2 teaspoons of flat white
- ½ in. squeeze of raw sienna
- ¼ in. squeeze of cadmium scarlet
- a dash of black to tone down the color
- a few drops of linseed oil
- 2 tablespoons of mineral spirits to thin the glaze to the consistency of milk

2. Test the glaze on the object for color and consistency. By trial and error, I arrived at the mixture on the far left of this picture. The mixture in the middle was too strong an orange, so I added a little flat white. This had the effect, however, of tinting it a gray blue (see mixture on the right), and so I added a little raw sienna and a speck of black in order to soften and age the color.

3. Apply the mixture with a 2 inch glazing brush. As usual, begin at the top and work downward. The width of the brush enables you to cover quite a large area of the surface in one stroke. Apply the paint thinly and evenly to one shelf at a time. As soon as you have finished each surface, drag the brush back through the paint without reloading the brush.

4. If you are less than 100 per cent confident of your dexterity, apply a coat of clear eggshell varnish and leave to dry overnight.

5. Take the original coral-pink glaze (see step 1) and darken it by adding:
- ⅛ in. squeeze of burnt sienna
- ⅛ in. squeeze more of raw sienna

6. Test the color on the object and, when you are satisfied, apply the glaze quickly and evenly to one of the columns with a No. 8 fitch brush. Finish off the top and bottom neatly so that you don't cover the capital or the pedestal. One tip is to paint the extremities of the column first with a sable brush.

7. Rumple a piece of cotton rag in your hand and dab it onto the wet glazed column to create a roughly textured background. Then, apply the paint to the next column and rag. Repeat the process on each of the columns in turn, glazing and ragging as you go.

8. Pour some of the glaze (step 5) onto a plate and add:
- a little squeeze of burnt sienna
- a speck of black
- a drop or two of mineral spirits to loosen the mixture

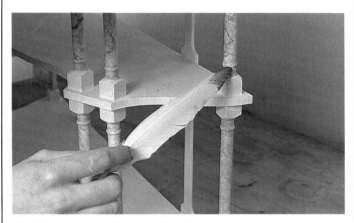

9. Dip a goose feather into this slightly darker mixture and, lightly and sparingly, apply some veins to the marble. Sometimes use just the tip and sometimes the side of the feather to achieve a varied pattern, emphasizing some areas and ignoring others. Because the columns are so narrow, you should aim to create a general impression of veining, circuiting the columns with the feather a few times—but not always in the same direction.

10. Dip a No. 5 or a No. 6 sable brush into the same, slightly darker mixture and pick out the lines along the rim of the shelves neatly and evenly. With a No. 4 sable, pick out decorative features, such as the acorns and the bases, to balance the overall effect. Once again, wipe away any mistakes with a rag dampened with mineral spirits.

11. Leave to dry overnight and then apply clear eggshell varnish.

Nursery Chair with Painted Ducks

Time: 2½ hours spread over 3 days; 20 minutes for varnishing on the following day.

Getting ready: If the chair is already painted, rub it down with sandpaper and wipe with a rag and mineral spirits. Apply two coats of white semigloss tinted a soft, pale yellow with raw sienna and lemon chrome.

STEP-BY-STEP RECIPE

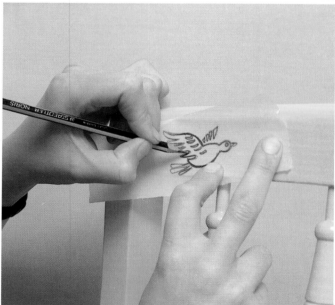

1. Trace the design onto a piece of tracing paper with an HB pencil. I liked this image of flying ducks I saw on some curtains. Remember that, when you turn the piece of tracing paper over and transfer the image onto the chair with a 2H pencil, the duck will fly in the opposite direction (e.g. left to right rather than right to left). If you want the duck to fly in the same direction, you will have to turn the tracing paper over and trace the image onto the other side with an HB pencil (so that there are now HB pencil lines on both sides); then turn the piece of paper back over again and transfer the image with a 2H pencil.

2. Mix a greeny blue glaze, consisting of a few drops of varnish with ultramarine, raw sienna and viridian.

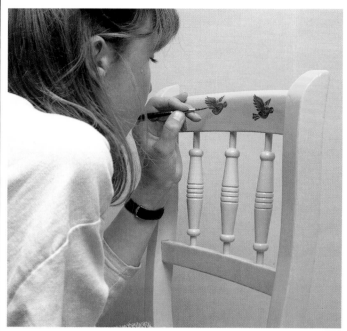

3. Take a No. 4 sable brush and, being as economical with your brush strokes as possible, paint between the pencil lines. Hold the brush upright, painting with the tip, and use your little finger as a support. Begin with the far wing, then do the body and, finally, the nearside wing. Don't worry if you paint over the lines; simply wipe away the whole duck with a rag and mineral spirits, dry the surface and begin again. Inevitably, the paint will lie slightly heavier and darker toward the sides of each brush stroke. But this will also suggest the form of the bird by giving a bit of dimension and an illusion of shadows and markings.

4. Mix a greener glaze for the bulrushes, consisting of raw sienna, viridian, lemon chrome and a drop of varnish. Make sure that your No. 4 sable brush has a firm, fine point and apply each of the bulrushes with a single upward flick of the brush, beginning at the base and tapering away toward the tip. Vary the arrangement of the bulrushes and make them bend a little, as if blown by the wind.

HANDY HINTS

When picking out, use features that already exist rather than invent new ones. However, if a piece of furniture has a lot of molded features, don't attempt to pick all of them out; choose either the convex or concave moldings, for example, and concentrate on these.

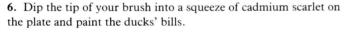

5. Mix a brown glaze, consisting of raw sienna and a speck of black, thinned with a drop of mineral spirits. Apply blobs of paint like husks of corn to the tips of the bulrushes.

6. Dip the tip of your brush into a squeeze of cadmium scarlet on the plate and paint the ducks' bills.

7. Pick out some of the chair's existing moldings—in this case, the convex moldings—in the color you used for the bodies of the ducks (see step 2). You might also like to paint existing features on the legs of the chair. Leave to dry overnight.

8. Apply a coat of eggshell varnish to all the decorated areas.

STENCILS

STENCILED patterns add color and decoration to both the structural features of a room and its furniture. They lend themselves particularly to borders running around a room or a fireplace, but they can also be repeated all over an object.

Since the cutting of the stencil is the slowest and trickiest part of the process, simple designs are the safest. They also look the most effective, especially when painted in bright, strong colors. The best stenciled designs are generally somewhat naive and rustic in appearance.

Once you have cut the stencil, the application of the design takes little time and uses very little paint. You can then bring some spontaneity and movement to the basic pattern by adding a little freehand brushwork.

Preparing the stencil

The recipes described in the following pages all involve the cutting of stencils. For this, you can use either ready-made stencil paper or sheet acetate. Or you can make your own stencil paper. Apply a coat of acrylic gloss medium and varnish to one side of a piece of medium-weight cartridge paper (150 or 175 gsm) and leave it to dry for about 10 minutes. The acrylic gloss medium and varnish will stiffen the cartridge paper; don't use cartridge paper that is any thicker or it will become hard to use. Draw the pattern on the uncoated side of the cartridge paper with a 2H pencil and then coat this side with acrylic gloss medium and varnish. Leave to dry for 10 minutes and trim your stencil paper to the width of the surface to be stenciled.

Materials (from left to right):
- Varnish or flat white as a medium for the glaze
- Acrylic gloss medium and varnish
- Oil colors
- Mineral spirits

Tools (from left to right):
- Cutting board on which to cut the stencil
- Mediumweight cartridge paper which you can then convert into stencil paper by applying acrylic gloss medium and varnish, or sheet acetate, or stencil paper
- Ruler
- Pencils (HB and 2H)
- Scalpel or craft knife
- Eraser
- Pair of scissors
- Tracing paper
- Sponge for applying the paint

- Plate
- Hole punch—occasionally useful for cutting round holes in the stencil paper
- Stencil brush
- Old paintbrush for applying the acrylic gloss medium and varnish and for mixing the paint

Stencil Floor Border

Time: ¾ hour to apply the stencil to about 10 feet of floor board.

Sources and applications: I took my inspiration for this stencil—a simple arrow design—from the pattern on the carpet and repeated it on the floor boards around the hearth. But a similar design would also have suited the edge of a wall, a cupboard or a chest of drawers in a room with a slightly rustic atmosphere. It would not, for example, suit a Regency-style room in a country house.

Getting ready: The floor should be varnished to prevent the paint from sinking into the raw wood. Wipe away any wax polish or grease with a rag and mineral spirits.

STEP-BY-STEP RECIPE

1. Trace half of the pattern onto the left-hand half of a piece of tracing paper with an HB pencil. Fold the left-hand half of the tracing paper behind the right-hand half and then trace the pattern through onto the right-hand half to create a symmetrical design. Repeat one component of the original design—a triangle, in this case—which will act as a register for the repeats.

2. Transfer the design on the tracing paper onto a piece of stencil paper with a 2H pencil. Make sure that the pattern is in the middle of the piece of stencil paper—in this case, I left a border of about 1½ inches on either side—so that, when reversed, the stencil is the same distance from the edge of the hearth. Then cut the stencil with a scalpel.

3. Try to choose colors for the stencil that complement those in the room. In this case, I mixed a grayish blue to relate the blue in the rug with the gray of the slate and which contrasted with the red in the room. This mixture, sufficient for about 10 feet of stenciled pattern, consisted of:
- 1 teaspoon of flat white
- 1 teaspoon of eggshell varnish
- ½ in. squeeze of ultramarine
- ¼ in. squeeze of raw umber

4. Pour the mixture from the cup onto a plate. Take a 1 inch stencil brush, dip it into the mixture and dab off any surplus paint on the side of the plate. Then, holding the stencil paper tightly against the floor with one hand (if you like, you can attach it with tape first) and holding the brush at right angles to the floor with the other, pounce the paint through the stencil paper onto the surface. You don't need to reload your brush often; a little paint will go a long way and, in any case, it should appear on the surface as a fine spray rather than as a collection of drops. Remove the stencil paper to test the strength of the color; although it may look very pale against the white paper, it will look stronger than expected against the darker floor boards.

5. Wipe away the paint from both sides of the stencil paper and turn the paper over—the symmetry of the pattern makes the stencil reversible. Using the triangle as a register, position the stencil for the repeat and repeat the process described in step 4. Leave to dry.

HANDY HINTS

Although there is some varnish in the original mixture, you should apply a coat of eggshell or gloss varnish to the stenciled areas for thorough protection.

The amount of paint you use is critical to the success of stenciling. Too little paint will leave a very faint impression; too much and the paint will bleed behind the stencil, leaving a ragged edge.

Positioning the stencil is most important. Cut the stencil paper to fit the area you want to decorate and then attach it with masking tape.

A Selection of Stenciled Boxes

Time: 1½ hours per box, spread over a couple of days.

Getting ready: Apply a coat of tinted semigloss to each of the boxes:

- For the PALE BLUE BOX, white semigloss tinted with ultramarine, a dash of raw umber and a dash of black.
- For the GREEN BOX, white semigloss tinted with viridian, lemon chrome, ultramarine and raw sienna to create a dark, clear, dandelion-leaf green.
- For the YELLOW BOX, white semigloss tinted a deep sunshine yellow with lemon chrome and a little raw sienna.
- For the PINK BOX, white semigloss tinted with cadmium scarlet and a little crimson and raw sienna.
- For the BLACK BOX, use either black semigloss or white semigloss stained with a lot of black and some burnt umber to create a deep browny black.

STEP-BY-STEP RECIPE

1. Draw a diagonal grid pattern, consisting of 1-inch squares on a piece of stencil paper about 12 inches by 8 inches. The easiest way to create this grid is to mark a series of 1-inch intervals from one corner along two sides of the paper. Connect these 1 inch marks to create a series of parallel, diagonal lines. Take one of the diagonals and mark it out into 1-inch intervals. At each interval, draw a line at right angles to the diagonal to create a series of parallel diagonals running at right angles to the first series.

2. Cut the stencil paper into strips so that there are at least two complete diagonal squares per strip. This will allow each strip to fit into the mouth of the hole punch.

3. Cut a base pattern on one of the pieces of stencil paper by punching six holes of the smallest size along each side of every square. On each of the other strips of stencil paper, punch one of several alternative patterns within the sides of the squares. These alternative patterns might include:

- A cross centered on a large hole with medium-sized holes at the four points. To ensure a clean and even break, press the hole punch quite hard and twist the paper free.
- A small circle at the heart of the square, surrounded by five larger circles.
- A star with four long tear drops radiating from a small central circle. Cutting curved lines with a scalpel is much harder than cutting straight lines. Therefore, when creating a tear drop or a petal, use the hole punch to cut a circular hole and then use a scalpel to cut away from this hole; the edge of the circle will give you your curved line.
- A flower shape with four petals.

4. Mix a thick, strongly colored glaze, based on paint and varnish, for each of the boxes:

For the PALE BLUE BOX, mix an off-white consisting of:
- 1 teaspoon of flat white
- a hint of raw umber
- a drop of gloss varnish

For the GREEN BOX, mix a golden color consisting of:
- ½ teaspoon of flat white
- ⅜ in. squeeze of raw sienna
- ½ in. squeeze of lemon chrome
- ½ teaspoon of gloss varnish

For the YELLOW BOX, mix a blue consisting of:
- a speck of white
- ½ in. squeeze of ultramarine
- ¼ in. squeeze of raw sienna
- a dash of black
- a brushtipful of gloss varnish

For the PINK BOX, mix a purple the color of red wine, consisting of:
- ½ teaspoon of gloss varnish
- ½ in. squeeze of crimson
- a dash of black

For the BLACK BOX, mix a browny red consisting of
- ½ teaspoon of gloss varnish
- ½ in. squeeze of cadmium scarlet
- ½ in. squeeze of crimson
- a dash of black

7. If you intend to apply the base pattern in different colors to several boxes, make sure you clean the stencil brush in between. Wipe off the old color with a rag dampened with mineral spirits and then rub the brush with a dry rag. Remember also to clean both sides of the stencil paper. Leave to dry for about 6 hours.

5. Take one of the boxes and pour some of the appropriate color onto a plate. Attach the piece of stencil paper bearing the base pattern (the six holes along each side of the squares) onto the box with masking tape. Begin with the sides of the box because the only places to hold the box are the top and the bottom which you should leave till last. Pick up some of the mixture on a stencil brush and dab off any surplus paint on the side of the plate. Then, pressing the paper tightly against the surface of the box with your fingers (you could wear very thin rubber gloves) so that the paint does not creep under the edges, pounce the paint onto the box through the holes in the stencil paper with the brush. Hold the brush at right angles to the surface—dabbing the paint on quite vigorously.

6. Once you have completed one area, detach the paper, wipe away any paint that has crept under the edges with a rag dampened with mineral spirits and attach the paper to a new area. The advantage of using a repetitive, symmetrical pattern such as a grid of diagonal squares is that the pattern itself acts as a register.

8. Apply one of the other stencil patterns between the crisscross grid you applied last time. Use the same technique as before and the same color, or the finished effect will be too fussy. Do the sides of the box first so as not to smudge the top.
Attach the stencil paper to the box with a piece of masking tape to provide extra support.

9. Take a No. 4 sable brush and, dipping it into the stencil color you used for each of the boxes (see step 4), paint around the molded rim at the top of the box. This will smarten the finished effect by obscuring the join between the competing crisscross stencils on the lid and the sides of the box. Leave the box to dry.

10. Apply a coat of semigloss or gloss varnish.

Ivy Leaf Stencil Fireplace

Time: 2½ hours for cutting and applying the stencil; ¼ hour for varnishing.

Sources and applications: I adapted this simple design from a photograph of a round tray on which painted ivy leaves twisted and turned to form a border. I decided to use it on a bedroom fireplace but, because it is quite understated in style, it would have looked equally good in a kitchen or in a bathroom. Depending on the color scheme of the room, you could vary the colors—painting the berries black or red rather than yellow, and the leaves a yellowy green.

Getting ready: Apply a coat of white semigloss or gloss to the fireplace and wipe down with a rag and mineral spirits when dry.

STEP-BY-STEP RECIPE

1. Draw a single leaf onto a piece of tracing paper. Cut another piece of tracing paper to the width of the stencil you want—in this case, the width of the fireplace. Transfer the original tracing onto the second piece of tracing paper with a 2H pencil. Turn the original piece of tracing paper over and transfer the leaf once more onto the second piece of paper, about ½ inch from the first leaf, creating a second leaf which tilts in the opposite direction. Even though the pattern consists of only two leaves, turn the original piece of paper over once more and transfer a third leaf onto the second piece of paper so that it tilts in the same direction as the first leaf. This will help you to register the pattern. Draw a stalk trailing between each leaf, but remember to leave a little gap between the stalk and the tip and base of each leaf. Otherwise, when you come to cut the stencil, the paper will be split down the middle.

2. Transfer the three leaves onto the paper with a 2H pencil.

3. On a chopping board, cut out the pattern on the stencil paper with a scalpel or a craft knife.

4. In a cup or can, mix a gray green to complement—rather than match—the yellow of the walls. For this room and fireplace, the glaze consisted of:
- 1 teaspoon of gloss or eggshell varnish (depending on the existing finish)
- a hint of flat white
- ½ in. squeeze of viridian
- ½ in. squeeze of raw sienna
- ¼ in. squeeze of black
- mineral spirits to thin the mixture to a creamy consistency

5. Secure the stencil paper with masking tape to a section of the fireplace, beginning at a bottom corner. Pour the glaze onto a plate and, bunching a piece of sponge between your thumb and fingers, dip the sponge into the mixture and then dab it on the side of the plate to remove any surplus paint. Begin to apply the glaze to the fireplace, dabbing the sponge firmly through the stencil at right angles to the surface. Never smear the paint on.

HANDY HINTS

Instead of drawing the berries freehand, you could have included them in the design on the original piece of tracing paper. You would then have needed to cut a second stencil, for two reasons. Firstly, it is very difficult to apply two colors (in this case, green and yellow) to a pattern using just one stencil; however careful you are, the second color tends to go through the holes cut for the first color. Secondly, while cutting holes for the berries, you might well have cut the stencil paper in two.

To cut a second stencil, place the first stencil (with its cut-out leaves and stalks) on top of a second piece of stencil paper of the same size. Pencil through the edges of the leaves and stalks onto the second stencil. Remove the first stencil and transfer the shapes of the berries onto the second stencil so that you can see how they lie beside the leaves and stalks. Take a hole-punch and punch holes through the second stencil for the berries.

6. When you have applied the paint to each stencil but before you remove the stencil and move onto the next repeat, gently blot the bottom half of each leaf with a cotton rag folded into a soft, smooth pad. This will lighten the bottom half of each leaf, creating the illusion of light and shade and of a third dimension. Imagine that the sun is shining from above and that the top half of each leaf is folded away from the sun, casting a shadow, while the bottom half of each leaf is folded slightly toward the sun, catching the light.

7. Gradually work your way around the fireplace; you will find that, as in a game of consequences, the third leaf, which is also the first leaf of the next repeat, will register the pattern.

8. Mix a glaze for the yellow berries, consisting of:
- a little eggshell or gloss varnish (depending on the existing finish)
- ¼ in. squeeze of raw sienna
- a dash of lemon chrome
- a dash of raw umber

9. Apply dots of yellow for the berries with a No. 4 or No. 5 sable brush, rotating the brush as if you were filling in the O's in a newspaper headline. Place one bunch of berries on the end of each length of stalk and position another little cluster of three berries, popping up from behind the leaf to obscure the fact that the stalk is not continuous. Leave to dry overnight.

10. Apply a coat of gloss or eggshell varnish to protect and seal the painting and leave to dry overnight.

Trompe l'Oeil Tin Trunk

Time: 3 hours spread over 3 days.

Getting ready: If the object is in bad condition, apply a primer and a rust remover first. If the existing coat of paint is in quite good condition, however, simply wipe it clean. Take a 1 inch decorator's brush and apply one or two coats of white semigloss, tinted a virulent green with lots of lemon chrome, some raw sienna and a little black. Leave to dry overnight.

STEP-BY-STEP RECIPE

1. Mix a glaze, consisting of:
- 2 teaspoons of the original undercoat
- 1 in. squeeze of viridian
- 1 in. squeeze of ultramarine
- ½ in. squeeze of lemon chrome
- ½ in. squeeze of black
- mineral spirits

2. Test the mixture on the object for color—the sort of dark green you might see on a leather-bound book—and for consistency—that of thin cream.

3. Apply the paint with a 1 inch decorator's brush to one surface of the trunk at a time, beginning with the lid.

4. Crumple a piece of rag in your hand and arrange it until the pad that you are going to place against the object is finely creased. Check that there are no dominant creases, such as a strong diagonal, because these will create a repetitive pattern. Blot the rag quite firmly against the glazed surface to leave a subtle, mottled finish that looks like a leather hide stretched over the trunk. Remember to vary the direction of ragging as you go. Compared with the crisply textured backgrounds often created when ragging marble finishes, this effect should be much softer. The variations in color between the undercoat and the glaze are less acute. And, because the glaze is thicker and therefore clings to the surface more tightly than with marbling, you remove less paint with the rag, creating less of a color contrast. Leave the trunk to dry overnight.

5. Apply a coat of eggshell varnish and leave to dry.

6. You might now like to stencil the edges of the trunk with studs and reinforced corners to simulate brass. Cut a strip 1½ inches wide from a length of stencil paper and pencil two lines—each ½ inch in from either edge—along the strip. These will help you to center the circles. Use a coin or the cap of a tube of paint to pencil the circles onto the stencil paper. Draw a trefoil for the reinforced corners on a separate piece of stencil paper.

7. Cut the stencils with a scalpel. Circles are some of the hardest stencils to cut; so, go slowly and smoothly, drawing the knife toward your body rather than away.

8. On a plate, mix a browny green glaze for the brass studs and the reinforced corners, consisting of:
- a brushtipful of the original semigloss undercoat
- a drop or two of gloss varnish to make the glaze shine
- ¾ in. squeeze of raw sienna
- ½ in. squeeze of raw umber

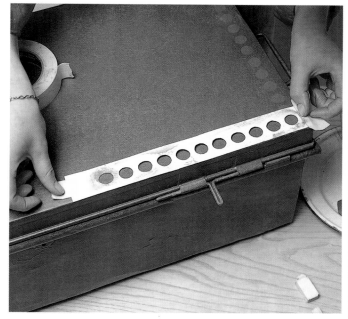

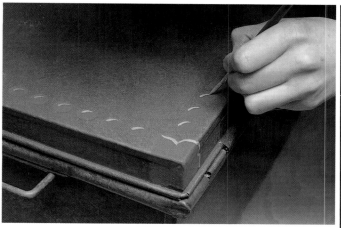

11. Take a No. 4 sable brush and, with not more than two slightly curved flicks of the brush, paint crescents of highlight *within* the top left-hand corner of each stud. You are trying to create the illusion that the rounded studs rise out from the surface of the trunk and catch the light on one side.

12. Mix a mud-colored glaze for the shadows, consisting of:
- a brushtipful of the mixture on the plate (step 8)
- ¼ in. squeeze of raw umber
- a brushtipful of black

9. Position the strip of stencil paper along the edge of the trunk, so that the edge itself will guide you in a straight line, and attach it with masking tape. Pick up some of the mixture on the plate with a stencil brush and dab any surplus paint onto the side of the plate. Holding the stencil brush at right angles to the surface with one hand and holding the stencil paper down with the fingers of the other hand, dab the paint repeatedly through the holes. Each time you detach the strip of stencil paper, wipe the back to remove any paint that has crept underneath because this will smudge the surface when you move onto the next stretch.

When you come to the corners, attach the piece of stencil paper with the trefoil design to each of the three faces of the trunk in turn, and repeat the process. One of the three lobes of the trefoil will then act as a register for the first of the circles on the next stretch.

Leave the trunk to dry for a couple of hours.

10. Mix a pale gold glaze for the highlights, consisting of:
- a brushtipful of white semigloss
- a brushtipful of the mixture on the plate (step 8)
- ¼ in. squeeze more of raw sienna
  Don't worry if this appears quite dark on the plate; it will read more brightly against the darkness of the studs.

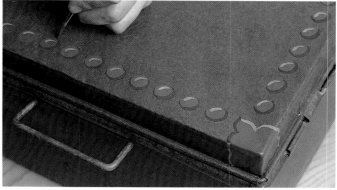

13. Paint crescents of shadow with the same No. 4 sable brush on the opposite side of each stud. The shadows are larger than the highlights and reach right down to the edge of the stud. The crescent is thickest at the point furthest from the imaginary source of light. Leave to dry overnight.

Stenciled and Decorated Dado Rail

Time: 1 hour for cutting the stencil and 1½ hours for applying the pattern to about 6 feet of dado rail.

Sources and applications: Stencils can be used to carry a theme suggested by a piece of fabric all the way around a room. Simply take a flower pattern or a motif from the wall-paper or curtains in your room and repeat it, using similar colors for the stencil. The added advantage of such an approach is that it's always much easier to copy or adapt an existing pattern than to invent one. In this case, I have picked up a pattern from the border of the curtains, adapted it and continued it along the dado rail.

Every time you paint something, you are adding to your personal library of ideas and experience. As a result, you will notice more and more how other people have decorated and furnished their rooms. You will become quicker both at spotting and solving design problems. For example, once I had stenciled the dado rail, I thought that the room needed anchoring, that there was too much color higher up and not enough down below. I decided to redress the balance by painting the baseboard black.

Getting ready: Apply a coat of white semigloss or gloss to the dado rail and wipe off any grease or dust with a rag and white spirit.

STEP-BY-STEP RECIPE

1. It is always easier to work out your stencil pattern on a piece of tracing paper first and then to transfer it onto the stencil paper rather than to try to get it right first time on the stencil paper. So, cut a piece of tracing paper to the width of the dado rail.

2. Place the tracing paper on top of the fabric bearing the pattern you are going to adapt and trace the pattern with an HB pencil. You may need to scale the pattern up or down to fit the size of the dado rail. Remember to begin the next repeat pattern so that you will have a key on which to register the stencil. Also, leave a plain border between the edge of the pattern and the sides of the dado rail.

3. Trace the pattern through to the other side of the piece of tracing paper with an HB pencil.

HANDY HINTS

Maintain an even pressure with your brush, making the lines flow as smoothly as possible.

Use the original pattern—in this case the border of the curtains—as a source of inspiration. But do not follow it too slavishly. It is extremely difficult to cut an intricate pattern with a scalpel and equally hard, when using a sponge or stencil brush, to dab the paint through tiny holes. Make your pattern simple, therefore.

4. Using a very sharp blade—a craft knife or a surgical scalpel—cut out the stencil on a piece of glass, an old chopping board or a cutting mat. Take great care to keep your fingers well away from the blade. You really could slice off the tip of your finger with it. Maintain a steady, even pressure with your hand, cutting around the design as smoothly, evenly and neatly as possible. Complete the large lozenge shape in two parts, leaving a little gap at each end; otherwise the center will be unsupported and will fall out.

5. Mix the colors to match or complement those on the curtain border. This will unify the color scheme of the room. For the red, mix in a cup a glaze consisting of:
- 1 teaspoon of gloss or eggshell varnish, depending on the existing finish. Eggshell is generally better but, in this case, the existing finish was gloss.
- ½ in. squeeze of crimson
- ¼ in. squeeze of cadmium scarlet
- a dash of black
- a little mineral spirits
  Pour a little of the mixture onto a plate. (These quantities should be sufficient for about 6 feet of dado rail.)

6. Start in a corner of the room or at a door or window. Attach the stencil paper to the dado rail with masking tape—securely, because you need to prevent the paint from creeping under the edge of the paper.

7. Grip a small piece of sponge between your thumb and fingers, dip it into the mixture on the plate and dab off any surplus paint. Then dab the paint sharply onto the surface of the dado rail through the holes in the stencil paper. You may think that the paint appears thinly spread and the impression looks pale. Once you have removed the stencil paper, however, it will look much brighter and stronger against the background of the dado rail. So, don't be tempted to use too much paint; it will creep back under the edges of the pattern and leave a furry, messy outline. Remember also to press the stencil paper tightly against the surface with the fingers of your non-painting hand. If some paint does creep behind the paper, you can carefully wipe away any intrusive little blobs with a rag. Alternatively, you could use a short, stubby, thick-bristled stencil brush.

8. Once you have completed the first repeat, detach the stencil paper, move it along the dado rail and attach it for the next repeat—taking care to position it horizontally. Because your original pattern duplicates the comma shape, you should find it easy to register this and all subsequent repeats to produce an even, flowing and regular pattern. Continue the repeats all the way around the dado rail, taking care not to disturb the paint of the previous repeat.

10. With flicks of the sable brush, add some teardrop-shaped leaves to either side of the stalks. Begin at the tip of each leaf, applying greater pressure in order to create a thicker line and lifting your brush away toward the base to make it narrower. It doesn't matter if all the lines and patterns are not identical because it is the differences which give the effect character.

9. Squeeze some viridian and a drop of gloss varnish onto a plate to match the green of the curtains and thin with mineral spirits. With a No. 4 sable brush, paint flowing green lines, like stalks, to connect the red shapes. Try to paint steadily with one continuous stroke of the brush so that the lines are as neat and natural as possible. If you are confident that you will not brush against the damp stenciled pattern, apply these lines immediately; otherwise, wait for the pattern to dry.

11. Mix a yellow glaze, consisting of lemon chrome, a little raw sienna to counteract the cold, acid effect of the lemon chrome, and a drop of gloss varnish. Thin the mixture to a workable consistency with mineral spirits and apply it with a No. 4 sable brush to the dado rail, creating yellow highlights to sharpen the overall effect. You might add a small circle of color on the inside of each petal, a border along the inside of each red lozenge shape or flashes of yellow to outline the edges of the flowers.

12. Leave to dry and apply a coat of eggshell or gloss varnish.

Rustic Red Stenciled Stool

Time: 4½ hours spread over 2 days for cutting and applying the stencil and for decorating; 20 minutes for varnishing on the following day.

Sources and applications: Decide on a collection of designs with which to decorate the stool. A piece of furniture as unpretentious as this lends itself to simple, primitive images rather than to grand, classical themes. I chose four simple patterns of flowers and of leaves, but you could find an infinite number of alternatives by searching in books or in nature itself for sources of inspiration. Each of the stencil patterns should be self-contained; you will apply each of them individually, gradually co-ordinating them into an overall design.

When painting flower designs, you might feel more confident if you search illustrations for inspiration and then modify the patterns. In this case, the star-shaped blue flowers are a little like periwinkles, the other blue flowers a little like harebells, one of the yellow flowers resembles a pansy and the other a rock-rose.

Getting ready: Apply a coat of flat white paint and rub down with sandpaper. Then, apply one or two coats of white semigloss, tinted pink with cadmium scarlet and raw sienna, and leave to dry overnight. Mix a glaze consisting of the same ingredients as the glaze for the little red chest on page 26 and apply it with a No. 10 fitch brush.

STEP-BY-STEP RECIPE

1. Draw the designs onto a piece of stencil paper—either freehand or, if you are less confident, onto a piece of tracing paper first. Bear in mind that you will have to cut these patterns later, so keep them simple, avoiding tight curves or intricate and angular lines. And remember that flowers are generally composed of an uneven number of petals, often five.

2. Cut out the patterns with a scalpel or with a craft knife (the scalpel has a narrower blade). Take your time and great care, keeping your free hand as far away as possible from the sharp blade. Finally, cut the piece of stencil paper into several separate pieces, each of which carries an individual pattern.

3. Choose colors to match the rustic image you intend to create. I decided on bright primary colors to perpetuate the primitive theme and to stand out against the strong red background, but I toned them down a little with raw sienna.

You can probably apply two of the colors—the yellow and blue for flower patterns—today, and the third—the green for the leaves—tomorrow. Mix the two colors for the four flower patterns in a separate cup:

For the two YELLOW FLOWER patterns:
- 1 teaspoon of eggshell varnish to make the color tough and translucent
- a dash of flat white
- ¼ in. squeeze of lemon chrome
- ½ in. squeeze of raw sienna to counteract the coldness of the lemon chrome
- a couple of drops of mineral spirits
- a dash of cadmium scarlet to soften the yellow and complement the red background

For the two BLUE FLOWER patterns:
- 1 teaspoon of eggshell varnish
- a brushtipful of flat white
- ½ in. squeeze of ultramarine
- ¼ in. squeeze of raw sienna to tone down the blue

4. Pour a little of one of the colors onto a plate, pick some up with a piece of sponge and dab any surplus paint off on the side of the plate. Test the color on the stool. If you are satisfied, take one of the stencils and, holding it tightly against a leg of the stool so that no paint creeps under the edge, dab the paint on the sponge firmly through the stencil onto the stool.

Repeat this pattern all over the stool—sometimes creating clumps of two or three flowers. Next, take the stencil for the yellow flower pattern and apply the same color to the stool—close enough to the first flower patterns as to hint at an overall design but not so close that the second stencil smudges them.

5. Take another piece of sponge and apply the second color to the other two flower patterns, gradually building up this overall design that will be knitted together tomorrow when you apply the third color—the green for the leaves.

Leave to dry overnight.

6. Mix a color for the green leaves, consisting of:
- 1 teaspoon of eggshell varnish
- a brushtipful of flat white
- ¼ in. squeeze of lemon chrome
- ¼ in. squeeze of viridian
- a brushtipful or two of black
- a few drops of mineral spirits

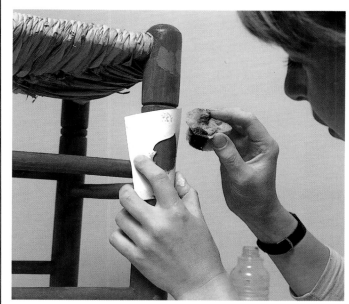

7. Take a piece of sponge (the two sponges you used yesterday will have dried, so you can use one of them) and dab it into the green glaze you mixed for the leaves. Next, take the leaf stencil and apply the leaves in the same way as you applied the flowers. Tuck the leaves in as close to the flowers as you can—it is this proximity which would have prevented you from applying them yesterday without smudging. Vary the direction and angle of the leaf patterns, occasionally applying a pair side by side to create a collection of little posies. Always make the leaves grow away from the flowers, rather than making them lie alongside. Look at old pieces of painted furniture for guidance in achieving the right effect.

8. Leave the stool to dry for about 6 hours. Because of the varnish in the mixture, it will dry quite quickly.

9. Mix a little black and raw umber and thin with mineral spirits to create a soft browny black. Take a No. 4 sable brush with a fine point and emphasize the outlines of the leaves and flowers. Be economical with your brush strokes, adding just a few thicker and thinner touches of paint here and there, to create a simple—almost primitive—character and charm.

10. Using the same paint, add stalks to the leaves so that they appear to emerge from behind the flowers, forming little bouquets. This will integrate the pattern. Next, give each leaf a central backbone. Begin at the base of each leaf with a broad brush stroke and gradually lift the brush away so that the stroke tapers to a fine point at the tip. Add the veins, staggering them either side of the backbone; look at a real leaf for inspiration. Finally, give some definition to the flowers themselves, outlining the heart and the individual petals which radiate outward from the center. Once again, the key is not to be too heavy-handed: to create an impression rather than something strictly formal.

11. Apply a coat of eggshell or gloss varnish on the following day.

HANDY HINTS

Applying the stencils to the stool is quite quick. The hand painting—the little flicks of the brush at the top of a flower or a leaf, for example—takes a little longer. But it is these that add the dimension which brings the finished effect to life.

If you make a mistake, simply wipe it away with a rag.

TORTOISESHELL

TORTOISESHELL is a tremendously smart finish. Traditionally it has been associated with rare objects and with inlaid furniture from the East; indeed, the fashion for re-creating it began with the craze for chinoiserie in the second half of the 18th century.

Tortoiseshell is glossy and sleek and slightly mysterious. To achieve this effect, the glaze is based on varnish for body and translucence rather than on white paint. The technique has gradually developed into a convention, but there is still a license for experimentation. The essence of the technique is to apply an even coat of strongly tinted varnish to an area of the object. You then brush this out to create the impression of a grain before stroking more color onto the surface with the side of a sable brush.

Sources and Applications

Tortoiseshell is found naturally in fairly small quantities or, at least, in smallish slabs. Therefore, the objects most suitable for tortoiseshelling are either small themselves or can be divided easily into several distinct panels. These include boxes, lampshades, tubs or jardinières, small tables or trolleys, wastepaper bins, umbrella stands, and mirror or picture frames.

Materials (from left to right):
- Mineral spirits
- Linseed oil to stop the varnish from drying too quickly
- Eggshell or gloss polyurethane varnish to give the glaze transparency
- Oil colors

Tools (from left to right):
- Tin plate
- A couple of fitch brushes for mixing and applying the glaze
- Sable brushes for adding the tortoiseshell marks
- 1 in. decorator's brush for tortoiseshelling larger areas
- Old can
- Tack rag for absorbing and picking up all the dust on the object
- Pencil for marking out panels
- Cotton rag

HANDY HINTS

Stand above your work in order to achieve a fuller perspective of the object as a whole. This will give you the freedom of working with all your arm—not just the elbow down.

Learn to judge the consistency both of the original varnish mixture and of the mixture used for applying the marks. If it's too wet, the marks will dribble. If it's too dry, the marks will sit uncomfortably on top of the background instead of sinking into the varnish. Therefore, allow the background to dry off for a few minutes before applying the marks.

Work quickly and confidently for a natural effect. Nerves show. Something underworked often looks better than something overworked.

Green Tortoiseshell Photograph Frame

Time: 1 hour.

Getting ready: Apply two undercoats of white semigloss, tinted sea-green with a little viridian and a little raw umber. The wood grain must not show through. Sand down lightly with very fine sandpaper to remove any bobbles in the paint.

STEP-BY-STEP RECIPE

1. In an old can, mix:
- 1 tablespoon of eggshell varnish
- ¼ in. squeeze of viridian
- ⅛ in. squeeze of raw umber
- a dash of black

2. Test the color on the frame. If it looks too much of a bottle green, add a little raw umber to make it browner and softer.

3. Brushing with diagonal strokes of a No. 8 fitch brush, apply quite a thick layer of the varnish mixture to the frame. Paint one side of the frame at a time, stopping at each miter. Make sure that each stroke covers the return on the inside of the frame, especially if the frame is to hold a mirror which will reflect the raw wood inside.

4. The curved surface of the frame might cause some of the varnish to drip; in which case, you will have to go back over it. Once you are satisfied, however, that the varnish has not dripped, leave the varnished side to set for a couple of minutes.

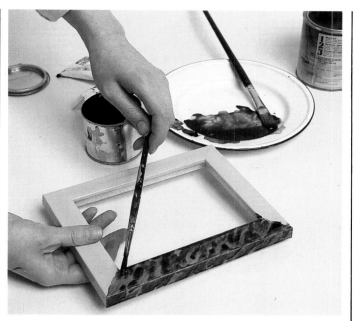

5. Pour some of the original mixture (see step 1) onto the plate and add a little viridian, raw umber and black. You can now apply the tortoiseshell marks to the varnished side with a No. 6 sable brush. Hold the brush at the end and, laying it flat against the surface of the frame, stroke in diagonal marks that fan out from the center of the frame. Use the length of the brush rather than the tip. Vary the direction of the marks; they should not all be at 45 degrees. And vary the colors by using more or less of the different pigments on your plate. More raw umber will give you browner marks; more viridian deeper green marks; and black will give darker, stronger marks. When you reach each miter, wipe the paint off with a rag.

6. Repeat steps 3–5 on the opposite side and leave to dry for 6 hours. Real tortoiseshell comes in slabs; if you were to paint two contiguous sides at the same time, you would lose the mitered edge that distinguishes the separate slabs.

7. Repeat the same process (steps 3–6) on the two remaining sides of the frame and leave to dry.

Brown Tortoiseshell Ice Bucket

Time: 1½ hours spread over 2 days.

Getting ready: Take a silver chrome ice bucket or wine cooler and wipe it down with a rag and white spirit.

STEP-BY-STEP RECIPE

1. In a cup, mix a strongly tinted glaze, consisting of:
- 2 tablespoons of gloss varnish
- ¾ in. squeeze of raw sienna
- ¼ in. squeeze of raw umber
- a speck of cadmium scarlet to brighten up the brown and make it look richer
- a little squeeze of black

2. Test the color on the object. If you are satisfied, apply the mixture to the whole surface with a No. 10 fitch brush, turning the bucket round as you go. Because the glaze is strongly tinted and quite thick, you should apply it quite thinly or it will get clogged up in the moldings—in this case, the grooves of the ice bucket.

3. Without reloading the brush, comb through the glaze you have just applied to give it a grain—running at an angle of about 70 degrees up and down the bucket. The grain is created by the bristles of the brush as they rearrange the coat of glaze.

4. Leave the glaze for a couple of minutes so that it begins to set. Pour some of the original mixture (step 1) onto a plate and add a little speck of black. Apply the tortoiseshell marks with the side of an old, fairly blunt No. 6 or No. 7 sable brush. These marks should follow the general diagonal direction of the background coat but, as always with tortoiseshell, try not to be too repetitive. Keep some areas quite empty and others quite dark and strong. Vary the sizes of the marks and the colors too—by varying the proportions of black and varnish on the plate. Leave to dry.

5. To give the effect a little more depth, mix in a can or cup a tinted varnish, consisting of:
- 3 teaspoons of gloss varnish
- ¼ in. squeeze of raw sienna
- ¼ in. squeeze of burnt umber

6. Apply the varnish with a fitch brush in the direction of the original tortoiseshell marks—that is, at an angle slightly off the vertical. The tinted varnish will give a more honey-colored finish.

7. Pour a little of the tinted varnish onto a plate and add some black. Apply a black rim to the ice bucket with a No. 6 sable brush. Try to keep the inside edge neat, wiping away any stray varnish with a rag.

HANDY HINTS

Remember to squeeze the pigments onto the side of a plate and break them up before adding them to the cup.

Tinted varnish kills two birds with one stone. It not only protects your painted finish but also, because it is a transparent medium, it can blur the sharp contrast between the color of the background and the color of the tortoiseshell marks, fusing them into a range of subtle tones. One of the problems with varnish, however, is that it's an absolute devil to get out of brushes. If you don't wash them well and immediately, it will set and ruin them. The other problem is that it collects dust very easily; so leave varnished objects to dry in dust-free rooms.

Red Tortoiseshell Lampshades

Time: About 25 minutes for a pair of shades.

Sources and applications: This effect is easier to achieve on small areas, such as lampshades for sconces or chandeliers, than on large areas where the varnish begins to dry out as you apply it. It looks particularly good on gold or silver chrome where the surface glows through the tortoiseshell.

Getting ready: In this case, the shades were made from hard, stiff cardboard sprayed with gold paint. The surface must on no account be porous.

STEP-BY-STEP RECIPE

1. For a pair of lampshades, mix in a tin a rich, browny red glaze, consisting of:
- 1 tablespoon of eggshell varnish
- ½ in. squeeze of crimson
- ⅛ in. squeeze of black

2. Apply the mixture quite thickly and evenly with a soft No. 8 fitch brush. Brush with diagonal strokes to achieve a good red stain which covers the shade yet allows the gold to glow through.

3. Leave the varnish for a couple of minutes to set. Varnish is a more fluid medium than flat white. If it runs, simply brush the drips back lightly.

4. Pour some of the original mixture (see step 1) onto a plate and add varying amounts of black and crimson. Pick up the treacly paint on a No. 6 sable brush and, holding the brush at the end, apply the tortoiseshell marks in the diagonal direction of the original brush strokes (see step 2). Lay the brush flat against the surface of the shade and stroke the marks into the varnish. Keep picking up more paint; if your brush becomes too dry, you will disturb the varnish underneath. Using your wrist, rotate the lampshade back and forth to check that the paint is not dripping. Leave to dry for about 6 hours.

HANDY HINTS

You could finish off the shades by picking out the top and bottom rims neatly with a little of the darker mixture (step 4) applied with a No. 5 or a No. 6 sable brush.

If you make a mess when applying the marks, wash the whole surface with a rag soaked in mineral spirits. Don't be afraid.

Flat or curved surfaces are the easiest and the most natural to tortoiseshell. There is little point in attempting the technique on a sharply molded surface.

Tortoiseshell Tin Tray

Time: 3 hours spread over several days.

Getting ready: In this case, the tray was already painted lime green with a darker green edge. To create this effect, apply a coat of semigloss tinted with lemon chrome and viridian.

STEP-BY-STEP RECIPE

1. Measure the tray to locate its center and draw a square panel in the middle. Extend the diagonals of the square to the circumference of the tray, thereby dividing the surface into four fan-shaped segments surrounding the central square.

2. In a cup, mix a dark greeny brown glaze, consisting of:
- ½ in. of varnish in the cup to give the mixture body and translucence
- ¼ in. squeeze of raw umber
- ¼ in. squeeze of viridian
- a drop of black (remember to break this up by mashing first on a plate or on the side of the mixing cup)

3. Test the mixture for color and consistency. It should be much darker than the undercoat but not so thick as to be hard to work with. Using a No. 8 fitch brush, apply the paint to the surface of the central square in a fan shape. Vary your strokes a little and allow the brush marks to show slightly, creating veins.

4. Taking care to break down the pigments thoroughly, add a little more black and raw umber to the original mixture on a plate. Only if the mixture has thickened (because it has been left standing for a while) should you thin it with a few drops of linseed oil and mineral spirits.

5. Pick up some of this darker mixture with an old No. 5 or No. 6 sable brush and, laying the flat of the brush (never the tip) against the surface, stroke the paint onto the central square. The original layer of varnish should take up the paint. Vary the colors, shapes and sizes of the marks so that there are no repeat patterns. Leave some areas quiet but make others quite busy. Be confident, quick and impulsive. Dithering will show. The aim is to create an appearance of random marks.

6. Don't worry yet about keeping within the pencil lines. When you are happy with the effect, however, then is the time to wipe away stray paint from the edges of the square. Tuck your thumb into a dry rag (at this stage mineral spirits will bleed into the tortoiseshell panel) and pull it gently toward you along the line. When the edge is neat, wipe along the line with a cloth dampened with mineral spirits. Since you cannot work on two contiguous panels in the same session, allow the square to dry overnight. Keep the original glaze in a cup covered with plastic wrap to stop it thickening and to protect it from dust.

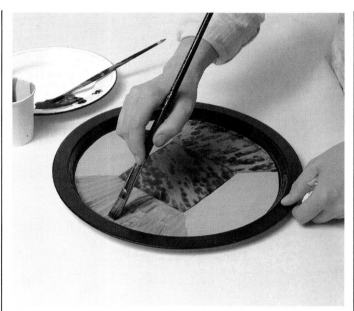
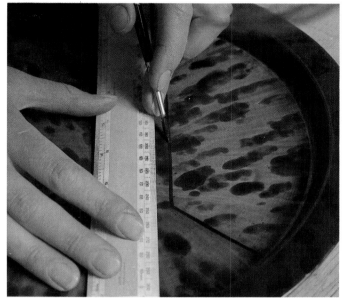

7. Repeat yesterday's process (steps 3–6) on two opposite segments, applying the paint in fan shapes with a slightly different orientation. Remember that you are creating separate slabs of tortoiseshell; if the patterns are too geometric, they will not look real. Leave to dry for 6 hours.

8. Repeat for the remaining two opposite segments. Leave to dry for 6 hours.

9. Add a little raw umber to the original glaze (step 2) to make it darker and browner. Apply this to the rim of the tray with a No. 10 fitch brush as evenly and thickly as you can.

10. Add some more black to the mixture—proportionately more because the background of the rim is darker—and stroke some tortoiseshell marks onto the rim with the side of a No. 6 sable brush. Imagine that the rim of the tray has been cut from a circular slab of tortoiseshell; the marks should therefore radiate out from an imaginary center.

11. Squeeze some black paint onto a plate and thin with a little gloss varnish. With a No. 4 sable brush, pick out lines, about ⅛ inch wide, between the five panels. You should still be just able to see the pencil marks which defined the central square and the four fan-shaped segments surrounding it. Hold the brush between your thumb, index and middle finger and rest either your fourth or fifth finger on the edge of a ruler to guide your hand. Drawing a straight line freehand, and without a ruler, in the middle of a circle is extremely difficult. Lining out will emphasize the illusion that the panels are separate slabs of inlaid tortoiseshell.

12. Line out the edge of the tray between the main panels and the rim. You might also like to apply a final black line to the very edge of the rim.

13. Leave the tray to dry overnight and, finally, apply a coat of clear varnish.

Faux Tortoiseshell Filing Cabinet

Time: 6 hours spread over 5 days.

Getting ready: Wipe the filing cabinet with a rag and mineral spirits to remove any dust and grease. With a pencil and ruler, divide each of the sides of the filing cabinet horizontally in two to follow the line between the drawers on the front.

STEP-BY-STEP RECIPE

1. Mix a sticky, honey-colored glaze by pouring equal amounts of eggshell and gloss varnish into a tin up to a depth of about 1½ inches (you could use semigloss alone but the gloss gives the varnish an extra shine). Stir in a 2 in. squeeze of raw sienna.

2. Apply the glaze with a 1 inch decorator's brush to one panel of the cabinet at a time. Brush the mixture on quite thickly with streaky diagonal strokes so that the impression of a grain emerges.

3. When you have covered one panel, pour a little of the original mixture (step 1) onto a plate and add some burnt umber and a little black. Take a piece of rag, bunch it between your fingers and, using it like a swab, dip it into this dark brown mixture. Dab blotchy brown marks onto the glazed surface, varying their arrangement but making them follow the general diagonal direction of the grain. Don't worry if, by this stage, the whole effect is looking rather a mess.

4. Take a badger softener brush and brush the surface very lightly, blending the marks into the background. At first, brush across the grain to spread the marks out sideways and, then, brush with the grain—but always so lightly that the brush strokes don't show. Remember to keep wiping the varnish out of the badger softener brush and to clean the brush with a rag and mineral spirits when you have completed each panel. Varnish, if allowed to dry, ruins brushes.

HANDY HINTS

Mash the pigments well so that they dissolve in the varnish without creating dark streaks.

Remember to tortoiseshell the sides of the drawers; these will be visible when the filing cabinet is open.

Stand back every now and then to appraise your work and decide which areas need building up.

Tortoiseshelling transformed this very ordinary cream-colored filing cabinet. However, if you have a red or a green cabinet instead, the same technique using false red or green tortoiseshell would work equally well.

Lining out requires practice and a steady hand. It is probably better to paint no lines rather than to paint wobbly ones. You could therefore line out just the frame.

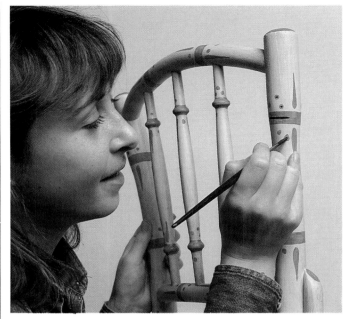

6. For the black lines inside the rings and spines, add ½ inch squeeze of black to the original red mixture (see step 4). The result will be a brown which will appear black against the red background but will not overwhelm it.

Use a No. 4 sable brush to paint fine, even lines, about ⅛ inch wide, around the center of each of the rings. Apply dots of the mixture to the middle of the eyes—large enough for them not to look like pinpricks but small enough to show the red around the edge. Draw a finer spine in the center of each of the original spines. The result will be a much sharper effect. Leave the chair overnight to dry.

7. Apply a coat of clear eggshell varnish or a tinted varnish if you want to distress it and make it appear older.

8. You could apply the same technique using different colors. For a chair with green bamboo rings (see step 4), mix:
- 1 teaspoon of flat white
- ¼ in. squeeze of raw umber
- ¼ in. squeeze of viridian
- ¼ in. squeeze of lemon chrome
- ¼ in. squeeze of raw sienna
- a dash of black
- mineral spirits

For a chair with blue bamboo rings, mix:
- 1 teaspoon of flat white
- ½ in. squeeze of ultramarine
- ¼ in. squeeze of raw sienna
- a dash of black
- mineral spirits

Add ½ inch squeeze of black (see step 6) to the appropriate mixture for the insides of the rings.

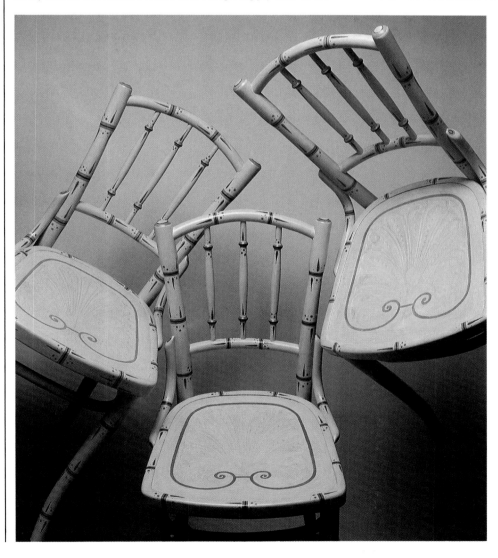

Bamboo Cycle

Time: 3 hours spread over 3 days.

Sources and applications: A bicycle, composed as it is of a series of struts, is a very good shape to bamboo. Many colors would look good, including yellow with brown and black rings or even black with red and cream features.

Getting ready: Wash the bicycle with soapy water and then rub it down with a rag and mineral spirits.

STEP-BY-STEP RECIPE

1. In a paper cup, mix a pale, apple-green glaze consisting of:
- 1 teaspoon of flat white
- ⅓ in. squeeze of lemon chrome
- ⅓ in. squeeze of viridian
- ¼ in. squeeze of raw sienna
- a brushtipful of black

2. Test the color on the object. If you are satisfied, apply ½ inch-wide bamboo rings at three or four inch intervals along the frame with a No. 7 sable brush.

3. Paint budding leaf shapes at the top and bottom of each stick of bamboo—the joints of the bicycle frame—and along the chain guard. Cover the mixture in the cup with plastic wrap and leave the bicycle to dry overnight.

4. The following day, make the original mixture (see step 1) a little darker by adding:
- ¼ in. squeeze of viridian
- ⅛ in. squeeze of black
- ⅛ in. squeeze of lemon chrome

HANDY HINTS

Hold your brush at right angles to the object to achieve clear, sharp lines and so as not to rub over what you have painted. It is essential to use two colors when applying the rings, spines and eyes. As soon as you start to add the darker, second color inside the first, the overall effect will begin to fuse.

5. Take a No. 4 sable brush and paint rings, about a third of the size, along the center of yesterday's rings (see step 2).

6. Using the same darker mixture, paint a spine down the middle of each of the leaves with three, four or five veins radiating out from the spine on either side. Then outline the shape of each leaf with the darker mixture, exerting more pressure on the brush at the base of each leaf and less at the tip where the outline should taper to a fine point. Try to keep this effect simple and natural. Leave to dry overnight.

7. Apply a coat of gloss enamel varnish. Since a bicycle will get quite a bit of wear, it must be very well varnished for protection. Mine has led a busy life in London without showing any signs of distress.

MARBLES AND STONES

MARBLE has the atmosphere of age and authority. It is the stone for cathedrals and churches or for royal palaces draped in damasks and silks.

When you recreate marble, you should aim to convey some of the same weight and period feel. But remember that the best marbling gives a room presence without people noticing it immediately. Use marble sparingly and with respect. Natural marble has such a wide range of colors and patterns that there is no need to bastardize the material. It should not be allowed to overwhelm the room. There is nothing worse than the mauves and sickly yellows and greens that you find on the walls of some shops and restaurants. The joy of marbling is that it is remarkably quick. All you need is a surface that has been prepared and undercoated.

You can then transform an everyday item, such as a cigar box or a filing cabinet, into something extraordinary . . . create marble benches for your garden . . . or revolutionize whole rooms. Think hard about the existing decoration and the effect you want to achieve. Marble can look dignified in halls or dining rooms but it can drown pretty pink-and-white bedrooms. In bathrooms, its cool surface and smart veins are reflected in the water, creating an aura of luxury. Keep glancing at a sample of real marble as you work. This will both spur your imagination and keep it in rein. The cardinal rule to keep in mind is that marble is a natural material created under mountain ranges as continents collide. Painted marbling should have all the quirks and oddities of the real thing.

Nero Marquina (see page 80). This is a town, rather than a country, marble which looks very chic on table tops, fireplaces and even on wastepaper bins. A dark glaze, consisting of black and burnt umber, is brushed onto a white undercoat. Veins are cut with a feather dipped in mineral spirits.

Bianco Carrara (see page 74). This soft, subtle and understated marble suits fireplaces, panels and the areas beneath the dado rail in country houses. A glaze, lightly tinted with raw umber, flat white and black, is brushed onto a white semigloss undercoat. Veins are applied with a feather dipped in black.

Malachite (see page 97). The color of which fantasies are made— and, in this respect, similar to lapis lazuli although much easier to achieve. Because it is such a rich color, malachite can be overwhelming if applied over large areas. It looks most ritzy on little boxes, lamps, pepper-mills and ice buckets. A glaze, comprising viridian, lemon chrome and black, is brushed onto a pale green undercoat. The swirling patterns of the stones are created with a flat brush—contrasting with paler areas where the undercoat glows.

Giallo Siena (see page 71). This marble adds age and authority to solid objects such as table tops, plinths and columns. A glaze, based on raw sienna, is brushed onto a white semigloss undercoat. The veining then requires two different techniques: one removes the paint; the other applies it. Little lakes and pools are created by cutting through the glaze with a feather dipped in mineral spirits. The pools are then connected by dipping the same feather in burnt umber and fidgeting it nervously across the surface.

Arabescato Cervaiole (see page 76). The color of this marble complements any creams, yellows and pinks that are already part of the decoration scheme. It works well on fireplaces, table tops, and even on freezers. A glaze, based on black and raw umber, is brushed onto an undercoat of white semigloss. Veins are applied lightly. Finally, dusting with a badger softener brush increases the contrast between the cloudy areas and the sharp streaks, and creates tension.

Travertino Rosso (see page 72). The stormy effect of this very masculine marble looks good on solid objects, such as columns, pedestals and lamps, or on small boxes. It is created with a burnt-sienna glaze brushed onto a pale, creamy undercoat. Because the color is so rich and powerful, this marble can take extensive veining—applied with a feather dipped in burnt umber and flat white until the surface resembles a slice of Italian salami.

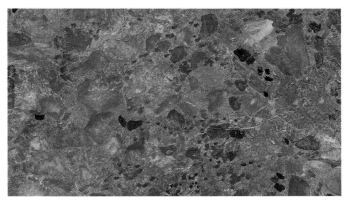

Verde Larissa (see page 78). A heavy marble with a massive Victorian feel. It looks equally good low down in a room—on baseboards, for example—and on prominent objects, such as lamps and tables. A glaze, containing viridian and black, is brushed onto an undercoat of pale green semigloss. The stones, with their jagged edges, are added with the side of a feather or a sable brush dipped in the original mixture plus viridian, raw umber and black.

Napoleon Tigre (see page 88). The naturally intense effect of this marble, which suits plinths, table tops and lamp bases, is achieved by varying the shapes, colors and sizes of the stones. A brown glaze, based on umber, is brushed onto an undercoat of beige semigloss. Each of the stones is then painted individually, using the side of a sable brush dipped in mixtures of black, raw umber, raw sienna and burnt sienna. A few veins are added with a feather.

Porphyry (see page 96). A solid-looking stone composed of many compacted particles of rock. Porphyry gives stature to small objects which have been crafted from it: small plinths, for example, boxes, obelisks, column lamps and pedestals. The effect is achieved by spattering color onto a ragged, red glaze.

Lapis Lazuli (see page 92). A rich blue stone composed, like porphyry, of tiny multi-colored fragments compacted together. Lapis lazuli is a semiprecious stone and should be reproduced only in small quantities, perhaps as an inlay on another marble. It gives a flash of rich elegance to obelisks, lamps, boxes, cabinets and candlesticks. This is achieved by spattering paint onto a glaze.

Materials (from left to right)
- Varnish
- Flat white paint as a medium for the glaze
- Linseed oil to loosen the mixture and keep it open so that it does not dry out too quickly
- Mineral spirits
- A range of oil colors

Tools (from left to right)
- A can or paper cup for mixing the paint
- A plate upon which to mix the colors and break down the pigments
- A couple of No. 10 fitch brushes
- A No. 4 and a No. 7 sable brush
- A couple of goose feathers
- A 1 inch decorator's brush with which to apply the paint and varnish large areas
- Badger softener brush

HANDY HINTS

Keep the glaze very thin. It may thicken as it stands uncovered, so thin it with more mineral spirits.

If the glaze looks lumpy and sticky after you have ragged it, it is probably too thick.

Don't despair if the marble does not work out first time. Wipe the paint away with mineral spirits and start again until you get the hang of it.

Marbling is usually more effective if you keep it simple and don't get overcomplicated.

Marble Bath Panels

Time: 1 hour for marbling and 10 minutes for varnishing on the following day.

Getting ready: Wipe the painted white bath panels with a rag and mineral spirits.

STEP-BY-STEP RECIPE

1. In a can or cup, mix a rich yellow glaze, consisting of:
- ½ teaspoon of flat white
- ¾ in. squeeze of raw sienna
- ¼ in. squeeze of lemon chrome
- a dash of burnt umber
- a dash of burnt sienna
- a few drops of linseed oil
- mineral spirits to thin the glaze to the consistency of thin cream

Remember to mash the pigments on the side of a plate before adding to the mixture.

2. Apply the glaze thinly and evenly to a panel at a time with a No. 10 fitch brush.

3. Fold a cotton rag into a smooth pad and rag the glazed surface gently to create a softly textured background (as opposed to the crisply textured background of the plinth on p. 78), allowing the undercoat to show through.

4. Mix a touch of flat white with some mineral spirits. Cut back through the glaze with a goose feather dipped in this mixture to produce a variety of wispy, rounded shapes rather than straight veins. Use the textured background as a guide, pushing the existing paint around with the side of the feather to create pale lakes and then pulling the feather away to its tip to define their edges. Because the mineral spirits make the mixture quite liquid, it may start to drip after a few seconds. Simply blot any drips with a rag, making some shapes even cloudier. Don't cut out too much; leave some areas of the panel untouched.

5. Mix some burnt umber with a hint of flat white and a drop of mineral spirits to create a soft, chocolate-colored brown. Apply very fine veins with a goose feather, sometimes outlining the pale lakes and sometimes cutting right through them. Leave to dry.

6. Repeat steps 2–5 on the remaining panels.

7. Apply a coat of gloss or eggshell varnish (depending on the finish of the original surface).

Red Sienna Marble Telephone

Time: 1½ hours for marbling and ¼ hour for applying the varnish the following day.

Sources and applications: This rich, warm marble is quite overpowering and looks best in small doses. It would look smart on panels edged in black or on a border for a paler marble.

Getting ready: Wipe off any grease with a rag and mineral spirits and mask the number plate with tape.

STEP-BY-STEP RECIPE

1. For this phoney effect, mix a glaze consisting of:
- a hint of flat white
- ½ in. squeeze of burnt sienna
- ½ in. squeeze of cadmium scarlet
- ½ in. squeeze of raw sienna
- a drop of linseed oil
- mineral spirits to thin the glaze to the consistency of milk

2. Apply the glaze to the whole surface with a No. 8 fitch brush. Use a No. 4 sable to brush the paint into the tight spaces between the push buttons. But try not to clog these spaces with paint.

3. Blot the surface with roughly rumpled cotton rag to create a crisp, crunchy background. Make sure that you get into all the moldings. Do the same to the receiver—but try to do this when you are not expecting too many telephone calls!

4. Pour some of the original glaze (step 1) onto the plate and add a little black, burnt umber and white spirit. Stir this slightly browner mixture with a goose feather and then pick out the veins between any interesting shapes that have appeared in the ragged background. Lightly fidget the feather, jerking it backward and forward across the surface, to create a series of veins that run in a dominant, perhaps diagonal, direction. Try to work quickly and confidently. And don't forget to apply veins in between the push buttons to prove that the whole telephone has been hewn from a single block of marble. . . .

7. Lightly dust the surface with a badger softener brush to blend the hard edges between the colors and to produce a deep, cloudy effect. Leave to dry overnight.

8. Apply a coat of eggshell varnish.

5. Add a dash of crimson to the mixture in step 4 to create a deep red for some more veins. Apply these with a goose feather, emphasizing the edges of the darker veins. Try to vary the width of the veins—using the feather on its side for thick lines and then pulling it away to its tip for thin lines.

6. Wipe the plate and mix a little flat white with a few drops of mineral spirits and a hint of raw sienna to create a creamy brown, which will read as white against the background. Apply some paler veins with the goose feather. If you had used just flat white, the color would have appeared glaringly white and out of place.

HANDY HINTS

Feathers hold very little paint and are, therefore, useful for applying light, delicate veins. They can also be used on their sides to push existing paint around. Experiment to get an idea of their versatility.

Trompe l'Oeil Paneled Freezer

Time: 3 hours spread over 4 days for each freezer.

Getting ready: Wipe the metal door of the freezer with a rag soaked in mineral spirits to remove any grease. With a sharp pencil and a ruler, mark out a central panel 4 inches in all round from the edges of the door.

Sources and applications: This marble finish—in particular, that of the pale inset panel—suits a variety of surroundings. It is quiet, natural and does not fight with the other colors. It can therefore be used to cover quite large areas. You could paint the walls of a whole bathroom with it or the panels in a kitchen, a fireplace in a sitting room or even pieces of furniture such as a dining room table.

STEP-BY-STEP RECIPE

1. In a can, mix a pale gray glaze, consisting of:
- 1 teaspoon of flat white
- ¼ in. squeeze of raw umber (to counteract the blueness in the white and the black)
- a brushtipful of black
- a few drops of linseed oil (you need only a little oil since metal is not absorbent, like wood; for a panel of wood the same size, you would need about ½ teaspoon of linseed oil)
- mineral spirits to thin the glaze to a milky consistency

2. Test the color on the panel. It should be a pale fawn gray. Bear in mind that, since you are going to remove some of the glaze later by ragging, the color will be stronger now than it will eventually appear. If you are not satisfied with the color, simply wipe it off with a dry cotton rag and mark out again any pencil lines you might have removed in the process.

HANDY HINTS

Choose the dimensions of your panels by eye. You want a reasonable amount of edge without diminishing the feeling of a solid block of marble in the middle. Genuine panels on doors are usually 3–4 inches in from the outer edge.

Painted metal is quite a good material to marble because there is no danger of a wood grain showing through and giving the game away. Make sure, when marbling on wood, that the surface is well prepared and well undercoated so that no grain is visible.

3. Apply the glaze quickly, thinly and evenly with a No. 10 fitch brush to the panel. Make sure that every part of the panel is covered with paint and that there are no bald patches. Since the paint mixture is so thin, it will flow gently downward; so start at the top. Try to keep the glaze within the pencil lines, but don't worry if you make rather a mess of the edges; it will look more genuine if there is a lot going on in the corners and edges than if you create a perfect little picture of marble in the center of the panel. The overall effect must be of a slab of marble hewn from an even larger block.

4. Scrumple a cotton rag into a soft but rough pad and, before the paint has begun to dry, gently pat the surface to create a paler, softer, more textured background. Begin at the top and work your way down. Change direction now and again and vary the way you dab the surface so that you don't end up with a repetitive print left by the marks of the rag.

5. Dip a goose feather into the original mixture (see step 1) and tentatively apply some veins, lightly fidgeting it over the wet, textured surface of the glaze. Use the ragged background as a guide to where to place the marks; so, when you see an interesting shape made with the rag, emphasize it by outlining its edge or by linking it up with another shape or by applying a vein right through it. The variety you can achieve with a feather is far greater than that achieved with a brush. To create a very fine, clear line, use the tip of the feather; to create a broader line, push the side of the feather against the painted surface. If one of the veins looks too strong and heavy or has started to run, simply dab it off.

6. Stand back and look at your work quite critically. Are you in the process of making a mistake? Where should the darker veins that you are just about to apply go? If you put them there, will they chop the panel in two? Or if you put them in those two places will they chop the panel in four? Does that diagonal look a little false? Answering these questions takes a bit of practice but, so long as you stay relaxed, you will soon acquire the knack of creating a random effect.

7. Pour some of the original mixture (see step 1) onto the plate, add a little black and loosen with a few drops of mineral spirits. Now apply some darker veins—emphasizing a few of the veins that you picked out in step 5. Keep the veins light and tentative, instead of plowing them into the paint. Be brave about leaving some areas of the panel fairly empty and plain; but be equally brave and decisive about emphasizing strongly veined and contrasting areas where there is a lot going on. The veins should have a general, slightly diagonal direction but avoid angles of 45 degrees. You can break the diagonal every now and then with a vein running in the opposite direction as though there is a crack in the marble but be careful that you don't create an effect that looks like a pair of tartan socks. It's very common to make marble look too crude or dramatic. On the other hand, the more variety there is, the more convincing the overall effect will be. And the quicker you work, the less danger there is of the marble looking labored and self-consciously patterned.

If you are painting two panels side by side, complete steps 3–7 on one panel before beginning the second panel; if the paint is allowed to dry, it will not push around easily and the feather marks will be hard to apply. Remember that you are creating two separate slabs of marble and you should therefore apply the veins in a different direction for each panel. If, on one panel, the dominant direction of the veins is diagonally from top left to bottom right, make the dominant direction of the other panel more horizontal, running at less of an angle from bottom left to top right.

8. Double or treble fold a piece of rag slightly dampened with mineral spirits. Hold it tightly between your thumb and index finger and, using your thumb to press it against the panel, guide the sharp crease along the edges of the panel, wiping as you go. Use your other fingers to keep the rest of the rag clear of the surface so that you don't smudge the paint. The edges do not need to be perfectly clean because you will later apply a coat of slightly darker paint to the surround which will cover the line. Leave the panel to dry overnight.

9. Apply a coat of varnish, consisting of two parts of eggshell varnish to one part of mineral spirits, with a 1 in. decorator's brush. This will protect the pale inset panel when you paint the darker surrounds. Leave to dry for 6 hours.

10. Add a little black to the original mixture (step 1) to create a darker, grayer glaze.

11. Apply this quickly and evenly to the surrounds, trying to keep outside the edge of the central panel. Since you have varnished this, however, you can always wipe away any paint that strays over the edge.

12. Blot the darker glaze with a roughly rumpled cotton rag. It is the impressions left by the creases of the rag that create the crisply textured—rather than cloudy—background. Move the rag around so that you are using a clean area each time rather than one which is soaked in paint.

13. Dust the surface in all directions with a badger softener brush to blend the paint.

14. Mix a hint of the original glaze (step 1) with more mineral spirits on the plate. Dip a goose feather into the new mixture, wipe any surplus mineral spirits away with a rag and use the side of the feather to create a variety of different shapes and veins. The mineral spirits will cut back through the darker glaze to the pale surface underneath. This technique of removing glaze with mineral spirits in order to create pale veins is the reverse of the technique you used to apply dark veins to the marble of the central panel (step 7). One is positive; the other negative. Dust lightly with a badger softener brush.

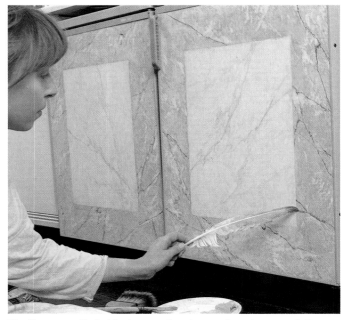

15. Squeeze a little black onto the plate and apply some delicate, darker veins to the surrounds with a goose feather. Outline some of the lighter shapes and veins, continuing them either side of the central panel to foster the illusion that the darker surrounds were hewn from a single slab of marble and that the central panel was then inserted within the frame formed by the surrounds. Make sure that you begin the veins over the edges of the marble so that there are no telltale stop-and-start marks.

16. Fold a rag in two, dampen it with mineral spirits and, with your thumb tucked behind the sharp crease of the fold, wipe the inside edge of the panel to create a sharp line. There is some margin for error in doing this because you will eventually apply a shadow and highlight line along the edge.

17. Apply shadow and highlight lines to emphasize the illusion that the paler panel is inset into the darker surrounds. Imagine that the sun is shining down on the freezer from the top right-hand corner, casting shadows where the return faces away from the sun (at the top and on the right) and creating highlights where it faces toward the sun (at the bottom and on the left). For the highlight lines, thin a little white semigloss paint with a drop of mineral spirits and apply a line about ⅜ inch wide with a No. 6 sable brush. Use a ruler to guide your hand in as straight a line as possible. You might need to go back over the two highlight lines once again to ensure that they are bright enough.

18. For the grayish shadow lines, add some black and raw umber to the mixture used for the highlights and apply in the same way to the top and the right-hand sides of the panel. Take the border between the pale panel and the darker surround as your outside edge, painting over the pale inset panel rather than over the darker surround; the shadow lines will show up stronger against a pale rather than a dark background.

19. Miter the ends of each shadow line, painting over the highlight line to create a sharp 45 degree angle at the corners of the panel. It is these mitered edges that will create the illusion of real shadows and will give the freezer a third dimension, where the pale panel is "recessed". The shadow and the highlight lines will also have the effect of tidying up the border between the pale panel and its darker surround.

20. Leave to dry overnight and apply a coat of eggshell varnish for protection. For a shiny finish, mix equal proportions of eggshell and gloss varnish.

HANDY HINTS

When marbling a large surface, paint and rag separate areas of the marble as you go. If you paint the whole surface and then rag it, the paint will begin to dry, stiffen and become hard to work with.

Marbled Plinth

Time: 2 hours for marbling; 15 minutes, on the following day, for varnishing.

Getting ready: Prepare the plinth. Apply an undercoat of white semigloss, tinted a pale sage-green with a little viridian, raw sienna and black. In this case, one coat was enough because the plinth was originally painted green. Leave to dry overnight.

STEP-BY-STEP RECIPE

1. In a can, mix a dark green glaze, consisting of:
- 1 teaspoon of flat white
- 2 in. squeeze of viridian
- 1 in. squeeze of raw umber
- ¾ in. squeeze of lemon chrome
- ¾ in. squeeze of black
- 1 teaspoon of linseed oil
- mineral spirits to thin the glaze to the consistency of milk

2. Apply the mixture evenly to one surface of the plinth at a time with either a 1 inch decorator's brush or a No. 10 fitch brush.

3. While the paint is still loose, blot the surface with a crumpled cotton rag to create a roughly textured background.

4. Pour some of the original mixture (step 1) onto your plate and add a little mineral spirits. Using the tip of a goose feather, stir in some more black and raw umber to create a stronger, darker green which will read as black against the glazed background.

The raw umber softens the color by counteracting the blue in the black.

5. Apply the veins quite boldly, digging the side of the feather into the background. Rather than feather fiddly little veins, you should try to create the illusion of great chunks of compacted stone. Add varying amounts of viridian, raw umber and black to the mixture on your plate so that some chunks are greener, some browner and some blacker. Push your feather into and around the moldings as well. The veins should not break at the moldings; they should form continuous lines and contribute to the illusion that the whole plinth has been carved from the same block of marble. Work quite quickly so that the paint remains wet enough to work with.

6. Lightly dust the glazed, ragged and veined surface with a badger softener brush, brushing in all directions. As you go—and certainly when you have completed this side of the plinth—wipe the bristles of the badger softener brush with a rag. This is most important because it will keep your brush soft and make it—your single biggest investment—last longer. If you allow the paint to dry on the tips of the bristles, the bristles will go hard and crack. If the paint has already begun to dry, however, or if you are using varnish, wipe the bristles clean with a rag dampened with mineral spirits.

7. To counteract the blurred effect produced by softening, add a few more chunks of stone with the goose feather. Since the feather cannot carry much paint, make sure that your mixture is rich with color.

8. Repeat steps 2–7—applying the glaze, ragging, feathering and softening—to each of the plinth's other sides in turn.

9. When you have finished, return to the first side, which will have begun to dry a bit by now, and have a good look at it. Decide where certain shapes might need emphasis and, using the mixture on your plate plus some extra black and viridian, paint on a few angular stones with a No. 6 or a No. 7 sable brush. In particular, try to fill any pale, empty, unfeathered areas in the existing background with clusters of stones. Lay the stones firmly into the background with the side of the brush. Vary the sizes, shapes and colors of the stones—making some greener, some blacker and some browner. If the stones begin to look heavy and streaky, blot them gently with a rag to remove some of the paint and brush marks.

10. Dust very lightly with a badger softener brush to blend the stones into the background. This will tone them in with the other colors and create the impression that they are set into the marble instead of standing out from it.

HANDY HINTS

Scruffy, old goose feathers can be quite effective for veining because they create more texture than new ones.

Keep standing back to appraise your work and to help you decide where to add extra stones.

Remember to continue the veins and stones over the moldings, creating the illusion of a single block of marble.

Black Marble Table Top

Time: About 1 hour for a small table.

Getting ready: Undercoat with white semigloss paint. Then sand down lightly. Rub over with a rag soaked in mineral spirits.

STEP-BY-STEP RECIPE

1. Mix in a can or paper cup:
- a brushtipful of flat white
- 1 in. squeeze of black
- ½ in. squeeze of burnt umber
- ½ teaspoon of linseed oil
- mineral spirits

2. Using either a ¾ in. decorator's brush or a fitch brush, apply some of the glaze to the table to test the color and consistency—it should be about as thin as milk. When you are satisfied, brush the glaze on until the whole surface is covered. If you are decorating a very large surface you can divide it up into panels. Hold the brush close to the bristles for more control.

3. Gently blot the surface with a scrumpled rag to create a cloudy, mottled background texture. You will notice shapes and patterns emerging and it is these that you will pick out and emphasize at the veining stage.

4. Put a teaspoon of mineral spirits, a few drops of linseed oil and a squeeze of raw sienna on to a plate. Dip a goose feather into the puddle of mineral spirits and oil and add a little raw sienna as you go. Holding the feather very lightly, fidget or flick the tip across the surface of the table to create the veins. The mineral spirits will cut through the dark glaze, exposing veins of pale undercoat underneath and the raw sienna will leave yellowish streaks. Keep reloading the tip of the feather from the plate; if the feather is too dry, it will simply leave scratchy marks. When applying the veins, pick out channels between the background patterns that have already begun to emerge and keep referring to a marble sample. Although the veins should follow more or less the same direction, they should not run parallel like the stripes of a zebra. The overall effect should be random. Make one area very busy, for example, while leaving another empty. Avoid chopping the surface into segments. Feel free.

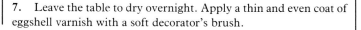

5. Holding a badger softener brush at right angles to the table, lightly dust the surface with crisscross strokes in all directions. Do not scratch. This will blend the different paints, softening the contrast between different areas of the surface and giving the marble greater depth. Keep wiping the paint out of the softener with a piece of rag.

6. To add some final definition and sharp focus, cut a few more veins with the feather dipped in mineral spirits. Stand back and look at the table to see which areas could be emphasized and which channels intensified. Be bold but don't overwork it. The important thing is to know when to stop.

7. Leave the table to dry overnight. Apply a thin and even coat of eggshell varnish with a soft decorator's brush.

Green Marble Mantelpiece

Time: 3 hours for marbling; ½ hour for varnishing 48 hours later.

Getting ready: A dark background generally sets off marble very well. So, to make sure that your marble mantelpiece will be shown off to its best advantage, apply a coat of flat black paint, thinned if necessary with a little mineral spirits, to the inside of the fireplace with a 1 or 2 inch decorator's brush. This will dry to a slightly chalky, old, soft, muted black. Apply a thin coat of flat white to the bare wood of the mantelpiece (if it is old and already painted, don't bother). Rub over with sandpaper. Next, apply two coats of cream semigloss.

STEP-BY-STEP RECIPE

1. In a tin, mix a rich green glaze, consisting of:
- 1½ teaspoons of flat white
- 1½ in. squeeze of viridian
- 1 in. squeeze of raw umber
- 1 in. squeeze of raw sienna
- ½ in. squeeze of black
- ½ in. squeeze of lemon chrome
- 2 teaspoons of linseed oil to keep the glaze open and to prevent it from drying while working such a large surface
- mineral spirits to thin the glaze to a milky consistency.

2. Test the color on the surface; the measures above are approximate. The paint should flow smoothly. Blot the surface with a rag to test the way the color will appear when ragged.

3. Because the mantelpiece is a relatively large object, divide it into three separate areas: firstly, one upright side; secondly, the top; and thirdly, the other upright side. Use a 1 inch decorator's brush to apply the glaze quickly and evenly to the first upright.

HANDY HINTS

Stand back from your work every now and then. If the pattern is becoming too repetitive, simply correct it with a rag and some mineral spirits.

If the mixture begins to dry out and becomes too stiff to move around easily, add a feathertipful of mineral spirits.

4. Then, blot the paint with a roughly rumpled rag to create a very textured background. Do the same to the top and the second upright. Make sure that you get right into the moldings and that you don't leave any collections of paint. Vary the general direction of your ragging. To protect the wall behind the mantelpiece, you could mask it with tape.

5. While the glaze is still damp, lightly dust the whole surface with a badger softener brush. This will rearrange the paint a little, blurring the sharp contrast between the dark green glaze and the pale undercoat that you exposed when ragging. Grip the brush toward its base, between your thumb on one side and three or four fingers on the other, and hold it at right angles to the mantelpiece so that only the tips of the bristles are in contact with the surface. Gently dust the glaze with short, crisscross strokes back and forth. Make sure that the bristles do not scratch the glaze, leaving their marks on the marble. If the bristles pick up a lot of paint, rub the brush clean with a dry rag. You can carry on using the softener for several minutes after you have applied the paint. But you will find that the longer the paint has been on, the firmer you will have to be with the brush. Keep an eye on what you're doing. Don't overdo it; if you do, the overall effect will be completely blurred rather than slightly out of focus.

6. Dip a goose feather into a thin mixture in a cup or can, consisting of ½ inch of mineral spirits and 1 teaspoon of oil, and apply broad, brave veins to the marble. Holding the feather at the end and more or less at right angles to the surface, fidget it jerkily to and fro across the glaze. Always begin and end a vein over an edge of the mantelpiece so that there are no stop-and-start marks in the middle. The mineral spirits will cut through the damp glaze back to the original cream undercoat. Begin on the first upright and then move onto the top and the second upright. The existing background will help you to decide where to apply the veins; you might want to outline a dark area or to emphasize a pale area by cutting right through it to make it even paler. Use the broad side of the feather, rather than just the tip, to create chunky shapes, rather than fine veins. Vary the amount of feather you use and the pressure of your hand, sometimes skimming the surface and sometimes pushing the feather right back to the undercoat. In general, however, try to give the veins a dominant direction. The mineral spirits has quite a vicious effect, like acid, but don't worry if the paint begins to run. With a rag blot any areas that dribble. And if the contrast between dark glaze and pale undercoat becomes too sharp, dust the surface lightly with a badger softener brush to tone down the effect. Leave some areas empty so that the overall effect is not too busy.

7. It is now time to add some darker veins in order to inject a little more drama—but don't overdo it. Add some black to the original mixture (see step 1) and, using just the tip of the feather this time, fidget it back and forth very lightly to emphasize and outline some of the existing shapes. You are now applying paint rather than removing it. Make sure that you go over the edges of the moldings to confirm the illusion that they too are part of the same slab of real marble. And vary the direction of the veins. Don't, for example, apply four diagonal veins running repetitively one on top of another like the stripes on a zebra's back. If the dominant diagonal on one of the uprights runs from top left to bottom right, make the dominant diagonal on the other upright run from top right to bottom left.

8. Leave to dry for two days (the oil in the mixture means that it takes longer to dry than most glazes).

9. In a cup, mix a dark bottle-green varnish consisting of:
- 3 tablespoons of eggshell varnish
- ¼ in. squeeze of black
- ¼ in. squeeze of viridian
- 1 teaspoon of mineral spirits

This varnish will both protect the mantelpiece and fuse all the colors together.

10. Apply thickly and smoothly with a soft, fairly new 1 inch decorator's brush. Brush in all directions, with crisscross strokes, so that the bristle marks do not show up in the varnish. Start with the top of the mantelpiece and work downward because that will give you a chance to catch any drips and will also minimize the risk of disturbing any areas that have already been varnished. Take care not to allow the varnish to dribble down the edges and collect near the moldings; it is a good idea to check these after about 10 minutes and to brush away any drips. The varnish will appear to age the marble immediately.

11. Leave to dry for about 6 hours. Finally, wax and polish the surface.

HANDY HINTS

Varnish fulfills two functions. The first is to protect the glaze. The second is to tone, or modify, the color of the original glaze. You will notice the toning effect of the varnish most immediately in the palest areas, which are now coated with a translucent greenish sheen. This gives the finish greater depth and fuses together the different colors that you have applied —the semigloss undercoat, the glaze, the light veins and the dark veins. Since the varnish will not carry very much color, you may need to apply two coats of varnish to tint an object quite deeply.

You need a good light for varnishing in order to distinguish— from the reflection of the varnish—those areas that you have varnished from those that you have not.

Marble Automobile

Time: 3½ hours for marking out and marbling; 45 minutes for varnishing on the following day.

Sources and applications: This marble has a modern feel. It looks particularly smart in hi-tec surroundings, complementing black and white.

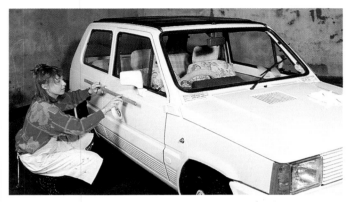

Getting ready: Wash the car thoroughly with soapy water and, if it has been waxed, with mineral spirits on a rag. Rub it dry with a clean rag. Mark out the panels for marbling with a sharp HB pencil. I decided to create marble panels on all the doors and on the hood, with a margin of about 2 inches from the edges of each surface. Scallop the corners of each panel, using the round edge of a roll of masking tape. Marking out is one of the most time-consuming aspects of this technique.

STEP-BY-STEP RECIPE

1. Mix a pink glaze, consisting of:
- 2 teaspoons of flat white
- 1 in. squeeze of raw sienna
- ¾ in. squeeze of burnt sienna
- ¼ in. squeeze of cadmium scarlet
- ⅛ in. squeeze of lemon chrome
- ½ teaspoon of linseed oil
- mineral spirits to thin the glaze to a milky consistency

2. Apply the glaze with a 1 inch decorator's brush to one of the panels at a time. Brush the paint in all directions, spreading it right up to the penciled edge. Do this quite quickly and don't worry if the paint begins to run; any drips will automatically be removed at the ragging stage.

3. Blot the paint quite roughly with a rumpled rag, removing as much of the glaze as you can and allowing the white background of the car to shine through. The aim is to create a slightly creased background texture which is paler than the glaze itself. Keep twisting the rag around in your hand so that the configuration of its creases does not become repetitive. Dab it extra hard around the moldings to ensure that the paint does not collect there.

4. Dust quickly with a badger softener brush in all directions to blend the creases into the background.

5. Next, apply the veins. Pour some of the original mixture (step 1) onto a plate and add feathertipfuls of burnt sienna, raw sienna and black. Vary the proportions of the different colors around the puddle on your plate so that the first veins you apply will be the palest, consisting mainly of the mixture plus a little raw or burnt sienna. Decide on a general direction for the veins and apply several quite quickly with the tip of the feather across the glazed panel. Stand back and take a look. How can you develop the pattern of veins? Emphasize some by making them thicker. Make some stronger by adding more black. Join a couple of the veins by adding a new one. The aim of all this is to avoid any hint of repetition by varying the angles, sizes, colors and directions of the new veins. Add some mineral spirits to loosen the mixture.

6. Dust the surface lightly with a badger softener brush, mainly in the direction of the veins. If you leave the surface for more than a few minutes before doing this, it will be hard to move the paint enough to blend them into the background.

7. Continue to build up the network of veins, adding more where appropriate. For example, you could follow an existing vein and, halfway along it, go off at a tangent, linking it with another network of veins. Add a little raw sienna, maybe, to give some veins a yellow tint and a little black to make others darker. For the sake of variety, try to leave some areas empty and to avoid creating series of parallel lines. Sometimes use the tip of the feather and sometimes the side, fidgeting it across the surface with confidence.

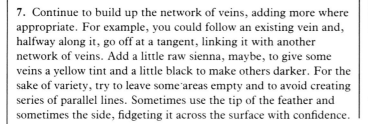

8. Fold a rag dampened with mineral spirits in half and, holding the crease firmly between your thumb and index finger, wipe away any paint that has strayed over the pencil marks.

9. Apply a coat of enamel gloss varnish or polyurethane varnish on the following day.

Napoleon Tigre Lamp Base

Time: 1½ hours to create the marble, plus 15 minutes for varnishing.

Getting ready: Apply an off-white undercoat, consisting of white semigloss and burnt umber to the lamp base.

STEP-BY-STEP RECIPE

1. In a can, mix a glaze consisting mostly of the earth colors:
- 1 teaspoon of flat white
- ¾ in. squeeze of raw umber
- ¾ in. squeeze of burnt umber
- a dash of burnt sienna
- a dash of black
- a few drops of linseed oil
- mineral spirits to thin the glaze to the consistency of milk

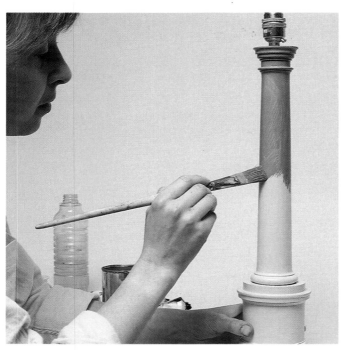

2. Apply the glaze thinly and evenly to the lamp base with a No. 10 fitch brush.

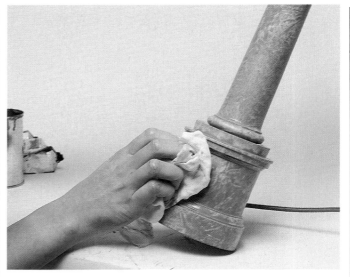

3. Scrunch a cotton rag into a rumpled pad and dab the glazed surface quite firmly to create a roughly textured background. Make sure that you work the rag into the moldings because nothing betrays false marble more than a build-up of unragged paint in the corners. Keep varying the patterns created by the rag.

4. Pour some of the mixture (step 1) onto a plate and add a little of each of the earth colors. Paint the stones onto the marble lamp base with an old No. 6 sable brush; the point should be fairly blunt. Hold the brush toward the end and, laying it flat against the side of the lamp, stroke it along the surface to leave irregularly shaped stones. Pick up hints from the textured background to help you place and shape the stones. Try not to repeat the patterns left by your brush because the stones should appear as random and haphazard as they would in real marble.

5. Try to vary the colors of the stones by using varying combinations of the oil stainers on your plate. Begin with gentler, lighter mixtures, scattering soft brown stones all over the lamp base. Then build up to the bolder tones in the following order (light to dark): Raw sienna; Raw umber; Burnt sienna; Burnt umber; Black. Apply some paler, sludgy gray stones by adding a litle flat white and mineral spirits to your plate; make these thin and translucent so that the undercoat shows through. Then add a little burnt sienna to the mixture to create deep red stones and apply these between the existing chunks. A mixture comprising black and burnt sienna gives a deeply purply gray. Continue to add increasingly dark and dramatic chunks of stone until they almost cover the undercoated surface. Whichever color you are using, apply it to different areas of the whole surface; keep moving the lamp base round to prevent yourself from concentrating on just one area. Add a little mineral spirits to keep the mixture flowing freely and evenly, but not so much that it drips.

HANDY HINTS

To create the illusion that the object has been hewn from one chunk of marble, make the stones traverse any mouldings.

Make the stones irregular in size, shape and colour.

Blot some of the stone marks with a rag to make them a shade paler and more subtle.

Occasionally roll your brush to leave a mark that looks like a rounded pebble.

If any of the marks threatens to drip, blot it with a rag.

6. Dust the surface softly with a badger softener brush, turning the lamp base around as you go and varying the direction of the brush strokes. This will blur the edges of the stones.

7. Add more of the original mixture (step 1) to the plate and add some burnt umber. Load a No. 10 fitch brush with this mixture and, holding the brush in the hand not normally used for painting, drag the index or middle finger of the painting hand through the bristles. The paint will fall onto the lamp base, spattering its surface and blurring the edges of the stones so that they appear less separate and distinct. You could also load your brush with mineral spirits and, using the same technique, splatter the surface with a fine spray which cuts through the paint you have just applied, exposing the undercoat beneath.

8. Add a little black to the original mixture on the plate to create a dark browny gray. Then, with the tip of a No. 4 or a No. 5 sable brush, paint small chips between the stones so as to define the edges once again and sharpen the overall effect. Make these chips sharp and angular so that they lodge between the stones rather than rest on top of them.

9. Add a little more flat white and mineral spirits to the mixture in order to create a fawn glaze, which will appear as white against the predominantly brown background. Dip a goose feather into the glaze and lightly tickle wispy feather lines onto the lamp base, picking out and emphasizing the existing veins or fissures between the stones. Leave to dry overnight.

10. Apply a coat of eggshell varnish.

Lapis Lazuli Candlesticks

Time: 1½ hours for two candlesticks, plus 10 minutes for varnishing.

Sources and applications: You are unlikely to find lapis lazuli in large quantities since it is such a rare and expensive stone. The effect looks more convincing, therefore, on boxes, candlesticks, obelisks, lamp bases, jewel boxes and hand mirrors than on large table tops or chests.

Getting ready: Apply a pale, blue-gray undercoat, consisting of white semigloss and small squeezes of ultramarine and burnt umber with a speck of black. Leave to dry.

STEP-BY-STEP RECIPE

1. In a tin or cup, mix a deep Wedgwood-blue glaze, consisting of:
- ½ teaspoon of flat white
- ¾ in. squeeze of ultramarine
- ¼ in. squeeze of burnt umber
- a dash of black
- mineral spirits to thin the mixture to the consistency of thin cream

2. Apply the glaze quickly and evenly to the entire surface with a No. 8 fitch brush.

3. Bunching a cotton rag into a soft pad, blot the candlestick to create a cloudy, textured background. The undercoat should show through the glaze in varying degrees.

4. Pour some of the glaze (step 1) onto a plate and add a squeeze of ultramarine to create a richer, deeper blue. Add a few drops of mineral spirits to loosen the mixture.

5. Hold the fitch brush in the hand that you do not normally use for painting and load it with the new mixture. Gently drag the middle finger of your painting hand through the bristles of the brush toward you and away from the object. Specks of paint will fall onto the candlestick in a fine, even spray.

6. Add a little mineral spirits, black and burnt umber to the mixture and repeat the technique in step 5, spattering spots of paint onto the surface.

7. Add a brushful of flat white and a speck of raw sienna to the mixture on the plate and spatter the surface again.

8. Add some ultramarine, black and crimson to the mixture and continue to build up the pattern on the surface with a final spatter.

10. You might also add a few lighter flashes with the sable brush. A mixture of flat white with raw sienna and a hint of black will appear white on the dark blue surface.

11. Leave to dry overnight and apply a coat of eggshell varnish.

9. For final definition, take a small No. 4 sable brush and dip it into the darker mixture used in step 8. Apply a few flecks of paint to look like larger chips of stone embedded in the areas that are least spattered. Make these chips slightly irregular in shape to contrast with the round spatters and to add natural unevenness.

HANDY HINTS

If you accidentally spatter too large a drop of paint onto the surface, lightly dab the area with a rag and go over it again.

It is difficult to control the spatters; cover up, therefore, and remove any objects in the vicinity.

Your fingers will get covered in paint when spattering; you could wear rubber gloves to protect them.

Granite Letter Rack

Time: 1½ hours to create the granite; ¼ hour for varnishing on the following day.

Getting ready: Apply one or two undercoats of white semigloss tinted a pale pinky gray with burnt umber and a little black. All traces of the original grain should be covered.

STEP-BY-STEP RECIPE

1. In a cup, mix a soft, slightly purple brown glaze consisting of:
- 1 teaspoon of flat white
- ¼ in. squeeze of burnt sienna
- ¼ in. squeeze of black
- ¼ in. squeeze of raw umber
- a dash of crimson
- mineral spirits to thin the glaze to the consistency of cream

2. Apply the glaze lightly and evenly with a No. 10 fitch brush to one area of the surface at a time.

3. Dab each area vigorously with a rumpled cotton rag to create a roughly textured background. Remember to press the rag into any moldings. The reason for ragging one area at a time is to catch the paint before it begins to dry (the glaze contains no oil to keep it open) and, thereby, to leave sharper impressions with the rag. Continue to apply the glaze to the other areas, ragging as you go.

4. Add some black to the original mixture (step 1) to create a cold gray color and thin down with mineral spirits so that the new mixture is only slightly thinner than the original. Holding an old No. 10 fitch brush with the hand that you do not normally use for painting, pull the index or middle finger of your painting hand back through the bristles of the brush so that drops, or spatters, of paint fall randomly onto the entire surface of the object. Try to achieve a range of sizes of spatter. The more mineral spirits you use, the runnier the mixture will be and the bigger the spatters. Don't worry if some of the big spatters run into each other and if the whole effect begins to look rather a mess. If one of the spatters really is too big, simply blot it with a rag, rumpling it back into the background.

5. Crumple a rag between your fingers and lightly dab the spattered surface—in some places pressing back to the original undercoat and in others simply blotting the spatters a little. This will create a cloudy background composed of three colors—those of the original undercoat, the glaze and the darker mixture. The joy of spattering lies in the variety of colors you can achieve—in about equal proportions—without disturbing the existing layers of paint.

Walnut (see page 109). A strongly figured wood with a swirling grain, walnut was popular with 17th- and 18th-century furniture makers, who used it in veneers and marquetry, before mahogany became so fashionable. Use walnut to give a feeling of relaxed confidence to any piece of furniture from a small picture-frame or a pair of chairs to a fine, inlaid dining room table.

Rosewood (see page 101). A slightly paler and brighter wood than mahogany with a less closely textured grain. Rosewood was much favoured in the 19th century by the Victorians who appreciated its quiet, easy-to-live-with appearance. It suits a wide range of objects: lamps and picture-frames, for example, chairs and tables, boxes and cabinets, woodwork and doors. Both mahogany and rosewood objects look even smarter when their moldings are picked out with gold leaf.

Ebony (see page 106). Due to the great weight and cost of real ebony, craftsmen have been attempting to re-create this dark wood since the Renaissance. Its close grain and its lack of color variation make it easy to imitate but do remember that, even if the wood has been ornately carved, the feel of real ebony is massive. Ebony looks majestic when picked out with ivory or gold leaf; you can also use it as an inlay on paler woods or on tortoiseshell.

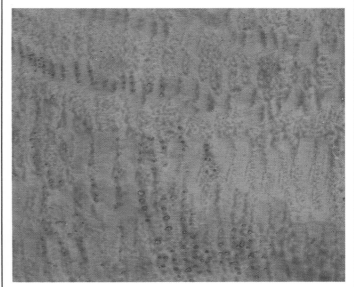

Faux bois clair (see page 104). This is a general term for pale wood-graining and is often applied to sycamore or maple, although a little artistic license is permitted to achieve a pleasing painted effect. Blonde woods look good on most pieces of furniture or woodwork, especially when set against blues, greens and yellows.

Pine (see page 108). A pale wood with a straight grain that is characterized by the occasional round, dark brown knot. Pine looks out of place in a classical setting but, when painted in a range of shades from a warm honey color to a cooler gray, it can contribute a rustic air to kitchen cupboards, dressers, blanket boxes, woodwork and floors. It can also make a good background for stencil patterns.

Materials (from left to right)
- White wax polish
- Varnish for mixing into the glaze
- Linseed oil to keep the glaze open
- Flat white as a medium for the glaze
- Mineral spirits
- A range of oil colors

Tools (from left to right)
- Masking tape for taping the brushes together
- Paper cup or can in which to mix the glaze
- Flat glazing brush (for applying paint to large areas)
- 1 in. decorator's brush
- 3 different sizes of fan brush (medium, large and small)
- No. 4 and No. 7 sable brush (on the plate) for adding detail to the wood grain
- A couple of fitch brushes (on the plate) for mixing and applying the paint
- Tin plate on which to break down the pigments
- Cotton rag

HANDY HINTS

In general, begin at the top when applying glaze and paint downward.

Think of the furniture maker when creating wood-grain effects and your painting will be much more natural and convincing. To decide which way the grain should run, imagine which parts of the piece of furniture would have been cut from the same piece of wood.

Rosewood Towel-Rail

Time: 1 hour, plus 20 minutes for varnishing on the following day.

Getting ready: Apply a coat of flat white paint to the raw wood, rub with sandpaper and wipe down with a rag dampened with mineral spirits. Next, apply two coats of white semigloss, tinted orange brown with burnt sienna, cadmium scarlet and raw sienna.

STEP-BY-STEP RECIPE

1. In a can, mix a glaze consisting of:
- 1 tablespoon of varnish
- ½ teaspoon of the semigloss undercoat
- 1 in. squeeze of burnt umber
- 1 in. squeeze of raw umber
- ½ in. squeeze of raw sienna
- ½ in. squeeze of burnt sienna

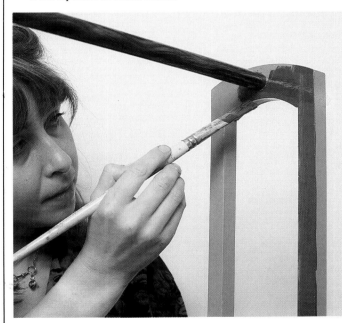

2. Apply the glaze thinly and evenly with a No. 10 fitch brush to a single part of the frame, trying to make a little paint go a long way. As you apply it, brush it out in the direction of the wood so that the undercoat glows through the glaze in subtle streaks that resemble a grain.

3. Having painted one part of the frame, apply the wood grain marks onto the damp paint so that they flow into and blend softly with the glaze (if the glaze has started to dry, the fan brush will scratch the glaze). To achieve this, pour some of the original glaze (step 1) onto a plate, add a few drops of mineral spirits to loosen it and add a little black from a squeeze on the side of the plate. Take a small fan brush (about ¾ inch across at its widest point), draw some of the smooth, dark mixture onto the brush and apply the markings to the glaze.

Imagine how the object would have been constructed out of various separate lengths of wood so that you apply your markings, or grains, in a natural direction—up and down the uprights and along the rails. It will help if you have a piece of real rosewood beside you; you will see that the markings can be wilder and more wavy than those applied when creating the subtle grain of mahogany.

Vary the way in which you use the fan brush so as not to create repetitive patterns. If you use its full width alone, you will simply create a series of parallel, equally spaced stripes or tram-lines. Twist the brush around in your fingers, therefore, so that you use just its side from time to time. Sometimes use more pressure so that the brush splays out and digs into the undercoat and sometimes use less, pulling it away very lightly so that the brush skates along the surface, leaving a paler, softer line. Temper your enthusiasm with restraint, leaving some areas of the glaze alone to create a contrast with the dark grain.

Vary the intensity of the color, too, mixing in more or less black from the squeeze on the side of your plate as you go. Remember that you can always add darker black marks, emphasizing certain areas, but it is difficult to remove them if you have applied too much black early on. Every now and then, add a few drops of mineral spirits to the mixture to make it flow.

4. Repeat the steps 2 and 3 on the other parts of the frame.

5. Leave the object to dry overnight. Three colors will be apparent in the finished object—the original orange-brown undercoat, the brown glaze and the darker, almost black, wood grain you applied with the fan brush. Finally, apply a coat of eggshell varnish to protect the finish. You can take this opportunity to modify the effect, if you like, by tinting the varnish—in this case, with some burnt umber to make it a darker, richer brown.

HANDY HINTS

When applying the glaze to each part of the object in turn, take care not to paint over the edge of a part that you have already grained.

Mahogany Chest of Drawers

Time: About 1½ hours; ½ hour on the following day for varnishing.

Getting ready: Rub the surface with medium-fine sandpaper to remove any lumps in the existing paint and to provide a key for the next coat to stick onto. Wipe with a rag liberally soaked in mineral spirits to remove any grease. Fill any dents in the surface with fine-surface filler and then smooth with sandpaper.

Mix a pinky orange undercoat, consisting of white semigloss, tinted mainly with burnt sienna, plus roughly equal amounts of burnt umber, raw sienna and cadmium scarlet.

Apply thickly and evenly with a 1 inch or 1½ inch decorator's brush, following the grain of the wood. The paint should be thick and opaque. Apply one coat if the existing paint is very pale; two coats if it is not. Leave to dry overnight.

STEP-BY-STEP RECIPE

1. Mix a clear, rich chestnut-brown glaze, consisting of:
- 2½ tablespoons of varnish
- ½ teaspoon of the semigloss undercoat
- 2 in. squeeze of burnt umber
- 2 in. squeeze of burnt sienna
- ½ in. squeeze of black
- ⅜ in. squeeze of crimson
- a few drops of mineral spirits to make the mixture flow and to counteract the stickiness of the varnish.

Mix the undercoat and varnish in a cup or can and add the pigments once you have squeezed them onto a plate and broken them down.

2. It is most important to test the color on the undercoat. What gives mahogany its depth is the pink of the undercoat glowing through the brown of the glaze.

3. When you are satisfied, apply the glaze thinly with a 1 inch decorator's brush to one entire surface at a time. The undercoat should gleam through the glaze; make sure that you don't leave any bare patches of pink. Use a No. 8 fitch brush for tight corners and for the stiles and rails. Work down from the top so as not to disturb what has already been painted. As you go, pull the brush back through the glaze in the direction of the grain you are creating—along the length of the top and the drawers and up and down the sides. The bristles of the brush leave a soft, streaky finish, like wood grain.

102

4. Pour some of the original glaze (step 1) onto a plate, add a squeeze of black and thin down with a drop of mineral spirits. Pick up a small amount of this mixture with a fan brush—about 1¼ inch wide—and apply it lightly to the wet glaze on the surface. The bristles are set in a head, or ferrule, which splays them out sparsely so that you can apply series of thin veins rather than a continuous coat of paint. Apply these darker veins—the grain—in fairly straight lines without scratching through the glaze. Keep picking up more paint as you go. Vary the pattern a little, turning and waving the brush to vary the width in contact with the surface: sometimes thick and sometimes thin. Make sure that you vein right up to the edges and use a smaller fan brush for the stiles and rails.

5. Repeat steps 3–4 on each of the other surfaces of the chest of drawers in turn and leave to dry overnight.

6. Add ½ inch squeeze of burnt umber to 2 tablespoons of eggshell varnish and thin with 2 teaspoons of mineral spirits. This tinted varnish will not only protect the finish but will also make it richer, softening the contrast in color between the palest parts of the wood and the darker grain. Apply the varnish smoothly and evenly with a 1 inch decorator's brush in the direction of the grain. Don't apply too much, or the varnish will drip and set in ribs where it has collected. Keep checking that it has not begun to drip; if it has, simply brush back through it. Because varnish is difficult to see—particularly against a shiny finish—it is easy to apply it badly. Be especially watchful with the molded panels on a door, where the varnish often dribbles down the stiles and rails and accumulates in the corners. Leave to dry overnight.

HANDY HINTS

To protect the finish and make it look, feel and smell even more like real mahogany, rub wax polish onto the surface vigorously with a cloth and leave it to dry for about 10 minutes. Then buff it up with a soft rag.

When wood-graining a picture frame, it is a good idea to pick up a color in the center of the picture and reflect it in the frame. In this case, having mahoganized the frame, I chose the color of the roof of the house and mixed a "toning" varnish tinted with cadmium scarlet to complement the foxy orange of the roof.

Bois Clair Mirror Frame with Ebony Inlay

Time: 2½ hours spread over 2 days; 15 minutes for varnishing on the following day.

Getting ready: Mask the edges of the mirror with tape so that no paint can creep under the edge. Apply two coats of white semigloss tinted a pale, creamy yellow with raw sienna and lemon chrome. Make sure that the undercoat gets into all the moldings and leave to dry overnight after each coat.

STEP-BY-STEP RECIPE

1. Mix a warm, slightly translucent, honey-colored glaze consisting of:
- 2 teaspoons of varnish to add body to the mixture without making it opaque
- ½ teaspoon of flat white
- 1 in. squeeze of raw sienna
- a brushtipful of raw umber
- a few drops of mineral spirits

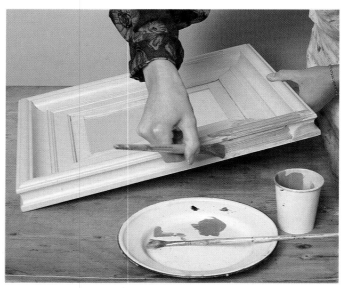

2. Starting at one of the mitered corners, apply this mixture to one side of the frame at a time with a No. 10 fitch brush.

3. When you have painted this side, go back over it, rearranging the paint without reloading the brush. Hold the brush more or less at right angles to the surface and press down on it so that its long bristles bend and splay. Twist the brush between your thumb and fingers to create swirls and tiny bubbles in the paint—sometimes the brush will twist right back over itself. Be quite firm and decisive; it may look a mess immediately but, within a few minutes, the varnish which has kept the mixture so easy to rearrange will begin to dry, settle and blend. Vary the pressure you exert on the brush—sometimes creating heavy accumulations of swirling paint and, at other times, lifting the brush gently away so that the side leaves a trail of light marks. Above all, try to create a pattern as random in appearance as nature itself. And don't forget the return!

4. Repeat the process described in steps 2 and 3 on each of the other sides of the frame in turn until you return to the mitered corner where you started. As you complete each side, check all the painted sides for dripping paint—especially around the mouldings where it tends to collect. If you do detect a drip, simply brush it away very lightly.

5. Pour a little of the original mixture (step 1) onto a plate and add some raw umber and a speck of flat white. Dip the tip of a No. 4 or a No. 5 sable brush into the mixture and place a dot or two in the center of each of the swirls of paint you have just created. These are the knots in the wood. To prevent the pattern from becoming repetitive, vary the sizes, shapes (not necessarily circular) and the positioning of the knots. You could have a collection of several knots very close to each other, for example, and then a wide area without any. Leave to dry overnight.

6. Using a small No. 4 or No. 5 sable brush, pick out a couple of the moldings (one at a time) in black oil paint, thinned with a drop of mineral spirits to make it flow. Try to exert a steady pressure on the brush with your index finger so that the bristles splay to a constant width, and use your middle and third fingers as a guide. Instead of being too timid at the start and then having to go back and fill in, it is better to apply the paint quite generously, wiping away any surplus.

7. Leave to dry overnight and, finally, apply a coat of eggshell varnish for protection.

HANDY HINTS

Complete one side of the frame at a time — both applying the glaze and the grain before going onto the next side. Make the mitered corners as neat as possible, taking care not to paint over a side that you have already completed. Remember that the frame consists of four pieces of wood, each with a distinctive grain.

Make sure that the paint is applied to the return of the frame.

Imagine that each molded side of the mirror frame was carved from a single block of wood, even if it obviously consists of three separate lengths. This will help you to fight the temptation of treating the moldings as tram-lines within which you create a series of rigid and repetitive swirls.

Instead, allow your swirls and your collections of paint to cross the moldings, thereby knitting each side together in one beautiful whole. You are imitating wood and not just creating a pretty pattern in paint.

Dark woods, such as mahogany, ebony and rosewood, look splendid when you pick out a molding in a light color, such as gold or ivory. These colors can look very weak, however, against the pale, honey-colored background of light woods, such as maple. For a smart effect, therefore, pick light woods out in a darker color such as black.

Picking out in black creates an instant smartness. But it requires some practice. It will help if you establish first what degree of pressure on the brush splays the bristles to the desired width; you then simply pull the brush along, maintaining the same degree of pressure.

Ebony and Ivory Record Rack

Time: 3 hours spread over 3 days; ½ hour for varnishing on the following day.

Getting ready: Rub the surface of the object with sandpaper and wipe it thoroughly with a rag dampened with mineral spirits. Apply a coat of dark brown semigloss; I generally use Vandyck brown. Alternatively, you can mix your own undercoat by staining white semigloss paint a dark browny black with burnt umber, raw umber and black. This can be a laborious process, however. Apply the paint thinly and evenly in the direction of the grain of the wood with a 1 inch decorator's brush. Begin in the middle with the insides of the shelves and work outward so as not to get covered in paint. Leave to dry overnight. Rub down with very fine sandpaper to remove any bumps in the paint and wipe lightly with a rag dampened with mineral spirits.

STEP-BY-STEP RECIPE

1. In a cup, mix a dark but soft black glaze consisting of:
- 2 teaspoons of varnish
- 1 teaspoon of semigloss undercoat (to create a soft black)
- 3 in. squeeze of burnt umber
- 2 in. squeeze of black
- mineral spirits to dilute the mixture to the consistency of thin cream
  Remember to mash the pigments on the side of a plate or a cup first.

2. Apply the glaze thinly with a 2 inch glazing brush to one surface of the rack at a time, beginning on the inside as before and working your way outward. Use a No. 10 fitch brush for tight corners and edges. As soon as you have completed each surface, pull the brush back through the glaze, without picking up any more paint, so that the marks of the bristles leave an almost imperceptible grain in the wood. If each of the surfaces is quite large, drag the brush back through the glazed area before you have completed the entire surface. Leave to dry overnight.

3. Apply a coat of eggshell varnish, tinted with black, and leave to dry for 6 hours.

4. To create the illusion of ivory set into the ebony, mix in a cup an off-white color consisting of:
- 2 teaspoons of white semigloss
- ½ in. squeeze of raw umber
- ½ in. squeeze of raw sienna
- mineral spirits to thin the mixture to a workable consistency
  Test the color on the object and modify the quantities if necessary. Don't worry if it looks a creamy beige in the cup; it will read much brighter against the black of the record rack.

5. To imitate an ivory inlay on the ebony veneer, take a No. 4 or a No. 5 sable brush and paint a line—about ⅛ inch wide—½ inch in from each of the four sides at the base of the rack. You can either pick out these lines freehand or mark them in first with a pencil and a ruler. Hold the brush between your thumb, index and middle fingers and pull it along the line, pressing against the surface of the rack with your middle and third fingers and using your little finger as a clamp or support. It will look neater if you paint the line in one continuous movement instead of going back over it again and again. When you have finished, however, go back over it once to even out any unequal distributions of paint. If you make a mistake, wipe it away with a rag dampened with mineral spirits.

6. Pick out the existing moldings in the same way. Once again, try to achieve as even and smooth a coat as possible by painting from one side to the other in one continuous movement rather than by stopping and starting, which will create buildups of overlapping paint. Finish off the corners sharply and cleanly. If the lines look too thin or gray, you may need to go back over the whole thing.

7. Leave to dry overnight and apply a coat of clear eggshell varnish.

HANDY HINTS

Because their impact is less immediate, it is always slightly harder picking out very light lines on a dark background than vice versa.

Pine Baseboard

Time: ½ hour per yard of baseboard; 15 minutes for varnishing on the following day.

Getting ready: Apply a coat of white semigloss, tinted a dull cream with raw sienna and a dash of lemon chrome, to the painted baseboard and leave to dry.

STEP-BY-STEP RECIPE

1. Mix a glaze, consisting of:
- 2 teaspoons of flat white
- 1½ in. squeeze of raw sienna
- 1½ in. squeeze of raw umber
- ¼ in. squeeze of burnt umber
- ¼ in. squeeze of lemon chrome
- 1 teaspoon of linseed oil (to keep the glaze open if the surface is large)
- mineral spirits to thin the mixture to the consistency of cream

2. Apply the glaze onto one stretch of the baseboard at a time with a 1 inch decorator's brush. Apply the paint quite thinly in the direction of the grain of the wood so that the bristle marks leave reasonably straight lines where the undercoat shows through.

3. Pour some of the mixture (step 1) onto a plate. Add squeezes of black, raw umber and burnt umber onto the side of the plate. Take a fan brush and, picking up varying proportions of the oil stainers, mix them into the puddle on the plate to create a muddy gray brown which varies in intensity.

4. Rearrange the existing glaze on the baseboard with the fan brush, adding a little of the new mixture as you go. The fan brush creates a streaky pattern which emphasizes the grain you had begun to create in step 2. Pull the fan brush in a straight line for a bit, then rotate it between your fingers to create a dark, swirling knot or gnarl before continuing along the straight line.

5. Add some burnt umber to the mixture on the plate to make an even darker brown. Hold a No. 4 or a No. 5 sable brush at right angles to the surface and paint an eye in the middle of each knot. You might also emphasize a few of the lines in the grain around the knot. Continue to build up the pattern until you are happy with it. The baseboard will be viewed only from a distance, so the overall effect can be quite impressionistic. Leave to dry overnight.

6. Apply a coat of eggshell varnish.

HANDY HINTS

If the mixture on the plate begins to dry, add a little mineral spirits to loosen it.

Look at a piece of real pine for inspiration. For a start, remember that pine trees are quite thin. Therefore, if you are doing a broad surface such as a cupboard door, try to create the illusion that it consists of planks of pine joined together; paint fine dark lines every 9 inches or so with a sable brush to separate the "planks".

When you need to discontinue a stretch of grain, lift your fan brush away very lightly so that the mark trails away without leaving an abrupt full stop. Similarly, when you start a grain, begin very lightly or at an edge so that there is no tell-tale mark that signals where you started.

Walnut Wastepaper Bin

Time: About 2 hours; 15 minutes for varnishing on the following day.

Getting ready: Apply a coat of flat white paint to the raw wood and rub down with sandpaper. Apply two coats of white semigloss tinted a rich, brown color with raw sienna, cadmium scarlet and a little lemon chrome.

STEP-BY-STEP RECIPE

1. In a cup, mix a glaze consisting of:
- 3 teaspoons of varnish
- a dash of flat white
- ¾ in. squeeze of raw sienna
- ¼ in. squeeze of burnt umber
- a few drops of mineral spirits

2. Test the glaze on the object for color (a sallow brown rather than a red brown) and for consistency (a little thinner than neat varnish). Apply the glaze to one of the panels with a No. 10 fitch brush. Work reasonably quickly because the varnish begins to stiffen within a few minutes.

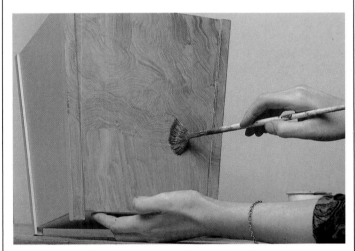

3. Take a medium-size or a large fan brush—about 1¼ in. across —and rearrange the paint that you have already applied. Without adding any extra paint, use the full width of the fan brush to create a strong sense of grain and direction—wood with a strong grain is said to be well figured.

HANDY HINTS

Keep a sample of real walnut beside you to spur your imaginaton. Although there is an element of fantasy in this finish, it is easier to start with nature and then to elaborate.

The advantage of the fan brush is that the ferrule splays the bristles out in such a way that each of the bristles leaves its own mark, thereby creating a grain. An ordinary brush, on the other hand, is designed to give a smooth, even finish in which the marks of the individual bristles are imperceptible.

---

4. Pour a little of the original mixture (step 1) onto the plate and add a little more burnt umber from a squeeze on the side of the plate. Pick up some of this fairly thick mixture on the fan brush and gently emphasize parts of the grain that you began to create in step 3, following the existing direction quite closely. This time, however, use the side of the brush rather than its full width to lay down the grain and sharpen the overall effect. Mix in varying amounts of burnt umber from the side of the plate to create different shades of dark brown. Vary the pattern, too— waving the brush lightly and exerting different amounts of pressure. Sometimes the marks will be quite heavy and, at other times, they will give the merest hint of a line as you lift your brush away from the surface. Be selective about the positioning of the grain.

5. Add a little more burnt umber to the mixture on your plate and, with a No. 4 or a No. 5 sable brush, paint the faults and blemishes into the wood. Emphasize a few of the knots and cracks that have already appeared to form. Place a dot just beside a dark collection of paint, for example, or outline one of the strong lines created with the fan brush. Since it is the faults that make a piece of wood look natural, try to avoid creating a repetitive pattern. Vary the sizes of the dots, or knots, and their spacing.

6. Repeat the process described in steps 2–5 on each of the remaining panels of the object in turn.

7. Leave the object to dry overnight. For protection, apply a coat of eggshell varnish. You may then want to paint the inside of the bin with a very dark brown or black semigloss paint to give it more weight, depth and strength.

Finally, a wax polish will create a soft, old-fashioned finish and a pleasant smell.

Maple Door

Time: About 2 hours for a door

Getting ready: Stripping previous layers of paint from a surface is a hard, and unnecessary, job. With wood-graining, all you need do is prepare the surface. Then apply an undercoat of cream-colored semigloss.

STEP-BY-STEP RECIPE

1. To maple a door, mix in an old can:
- 2 teaspoons of flat white undercoat
- 1½ tablespoons of varnish
- 1½ in. squeeze of raw sienna
- ½ in. squeeze of burnt umber
- ½ in. squeeze of raw umber
- 1 teaspoon of linseed oil
- mineral spirits

Break up the pigments with a stirring brush to get rid of any lumps and add them to the mixture in the can. With a fitch brush, apply some of the mixture onto the door to test for color—it should be pale, warm and honey-colored—and for consistency—similar to that of thin cream. It should be thick enough to stay on the door without dripping, yet thin enough for you to be able to move it around. The undercoat should show through.

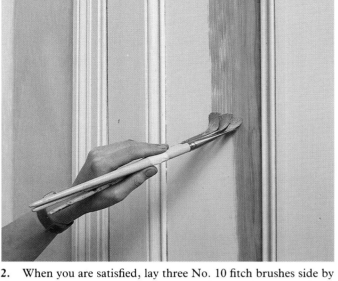

2. When you are satisfied, lay three No. 10 fitch brushes side by side on a table and bind them together with masking tape. The reason for using three brushes rather than one big brush is that, because the bristles of each brush follow a different pattern, they give the painted finish a greater variety. Apply the paint mixture to the door, a section at a time. The grain—and therefore the brush strokes—should run up and down the panels, horizontally across the rails and vertically on the stiles. Continue until the section is smoothly covered with paint and there are no white patches.

3. Without reloading the brushes and, holding them at 45 degrees to the surface of the panel, pull them back lightly through the paint. Don't scratch right through to the background. The aim is to rearrange the paint, buckling it in places so that it builds up into thicker, darker areas contrasting with thinner, lighter areas. Start at the top and work down toward the bottom and then slightly up again, avoiding heavy build-ups of paint at the bottom of the panel. The most important thing is not to leave any bare patches that would give the game away. Vary the weight of your hand so that the patterns never look mechanical (always remember that you are re-creating something that grew organically). If you are in danger of scratching through to the background, use more paint; but in general try to use paint that is already there.

HANDY HINTS

Keep samples of real maple beside you at all times.

You are always trying to achieve a balance between oil and white spirit. Too much oil and the glaze becomes thick, tacky and unpleasant to use and will not dry. Too much mineral spirits and the glaze becomes too thin and runny and dries too quickly.

SOURCES AND APPLICATIONS

You can gild a huge variety of objects: either by picking out existing moldings on lamps, boxes, tables and chairs or by inventing an inset line on any object with a flat surface. Once you are more adept, you can plan more ambitious patterns, such as gilded flowers and leaves, taking ideas from old pieces of furniture and toleware.

Even modest household objects can be elevated to a higher plane by the application of a little gold leaf. Add a flashing line of gold around a picture-frame or try it on painted baskets, peppermills or on a pair of candlesticks.

Gold goes very well with tortoiseshell, with dark wood-graining, such as mahogany, and with strong colors, such as blacks, blues and greens. It is less effective, however, with pale woods and with pastel colors.

New materials, new techniques
Gilding differs from the other techniques in this book in that it is not an attempt to create an appearance of something else; you are actually applying real gold. The materials you need are consequently very different.

Gold size
Gold size is a powerful glue, used for sticking gold leaf to the surface of an object. Once you have applied it, you leave it to set so that it will provide a smooth tacky bed for the gold leaf to lie on. If you don't leave it long enough and the size is still too liquid, the gold leaf will sink into the layer of size. If you leave it too long and the size dries out, the gold leaf will not stick down at all. Gold size comes in a range of types, each of which is described by the length of time it takes to set to the right stickiness and consistency: for example, one-hour size, three-hour size and twelve-hour size. I generally use twelve-hour size which means that I apply it one afternoon, leave it overnight and then apply the gold leaf the following morning.

Although it takes longer, the advantage of twelve-hour size is that it allows you greater flexibility and the finished effect is superior. The time that one-hour size takes to set depends to a large extent on the ambient temperature. If it is warm and dry, it might be ready in 40 minutes and have lost its tackiness within the hour. If it is wet, it might take longer than an hour.

Gold leaf
Buy a book of gold leaf, containing about 25 sheets backed by pieces of paper, from a specialist supplier. You may find that the price of gold leaf varies according to the price of gold that day. Gold leaf comes in a range of different colors that vary in tone and strength from acid yellow to bronze. I particularly like the slightly faded and old-fashioned effect of Versailles gold leaf. But I often use half-jaune as well. Given the grandeur of the finished effect, gold leaf is relatively inexpensive. However, even though it goes quite a long way, you will inevitably waste some of the gold leaf on the edges of the sheet.

Gouache
You can vary the effects of distressing by experimenting with a range of gouache colors. Burnt umber gives a good rich brown. Burnt sienna makes it red. And, if you want to make it more sallow and cool, use raw umber and/or black.

HANDY HINTS

Some people dust the surface of an object lightly with talcum powder before applying the size. This will prevent the gold leaf from sticking to any areas that have not been sized.

Make sure that your hands are clean before you start sizing or gilding; gold leaf has a tendency to stick everywhere that you least want it. Be as neat and precise as possible, even if it takes time.

Whatever technique you may first apply to an object that is to be gilded—whether it's marbling or wood-graining or decorative painting—always complete this process first. Varnishing kills the effect of gilding. Therefore, if the first process requires varnishing, always apply the varnish before gilding.

Oil gilding requires the use of an oil-based size; so, always wash your brushes with mineral spirits after use.

Gilding a Red Tortoiseshell Trinket Box

Time: 1½ hours spread over 3 days.

Getting ready: This box was originally undercoated with white semigloss tinted a pale red with cadmium scarlet, crimson and raw sienna. The background mixture for the tortoiseshelling consisted of varnish tinted with black and burnt umber. And the mixture for the tortoiseshell marks consisted of the background mixture with extra black and burnt umber.

STEP-BY-STEP RECIPE

1. Pour 1 teaspoon of white semigloss into a cup and tint it a warm golden yellow with ½ inch squeeze of lemon chrome and just over ½ inch squeeze of raw sienna. Pick out the rim and any moldings that you intend to gild with a No. 4 or a No. 5 sable brush. If you decide to initial the box, pencil or trace the initial onto the box first and then apply the paint. The advantage of applying this yellow paint is twofold: it will show you where to apply the size on the following day and it will provide a yellow background for the gold leaf, so that any areas you miss when gilding will be less apparent.

2. Clean around the edges of the initial with a cotton rag, sharply creased between thumb and forefinger. Leave to dry overnight.

3. Apply 12-hour gold size to the yellow areas with a No. 4 sable brush. Leave to dry overnight.

4. Cut the gold leaf into narrow strips and apply to the sized surfaces, including the initial. Leave the gold for about half an hour to set.

5. Rub the gilded surfaces gently with a dry rag to remove stray flakes of gold. Then, tidy up the edges with a rag slightly dampened with mineral spirits.

6. To tone down the brilliance of the gold, apply a little burnt-umber gouache mixed with water and a drop of detergent.

Gilded Mahogany Plant Tub

Time: 1½ hours spread over 3 days.

Getting ready: This tub was undercoated with white semigloss tinted orange with raw sienna and cadmium scarlet. It was then mahoganized (see page 102) and varnished.

STEP-BY-STEP RECIPE

1.   Apply the golden yellow paint (see step 1 on the facing page) evenly to the moldings of the mahogany tub with a No. 6 sable brush. Leave to dry overnight.

2.   Apply 12-hour gold size to the yellow moldings with a No. 6 sable brush and leave to dry overnight.

3.   Cut a sheet of Versailles (or half-jaune) gold leaf into strips the same width as the bands, or moldings, on the tub. In total, the tub will need about two or three sheets. Next, position the strips of gold leaf carefully against the sized surfaces. Rub against the backing paper with your fingertips and the gold leaf will peel off. Use a soft, firm cotton swab to rub the intricate spaces between the moldings.

4.   Leave the gold leaf for about half an hour to set before returning to tidy it up. Finally, apply a little burnt-umber gouache diluted with a drop of water and detergent to achieve a slightly distressed finish.

Restoring and Gilding a Black Bench

Time: 2½ hours spread over 3 days.

Getting ready: Rub the object with a rag dampened with mineral spirits to remove surface dust and grease. Mix some paint to match the black of the bench. Remember that a faded old object is seldom pure black; it is usually a very dark brown. Depending on how sallow or rich the color is, therefore, tint the black with raw umber or burnt umber. In this case, I mixed a little raw umber with the black and then added a drop of gloss varnish (because the original surface was quity shiny), a little eggshell varnish and some mineral spirits. The varnish both acts as a medium for the color, helping it to dry, and protects the finish.

Test the paint on the object with a soft No. 5 sable brush. Because the paint appears darker when dry, it is a good idea to test a small area quickly for color and glossiness by drying it with a hair dryer first.

Retouch all the bare areas, but don't overdo it. Leave the object to dry overnight.

STEP-BY-STEP RECIPE

1. Using a No. 5 sable brush, apply some 12-hour gold size to the moldings that will be gilded. Try not to go over the edges of the moldings. If you do, simply wipe away the size with a rag dampened with mineral spirits or the gold leaf will stick to areas for which it was not intended. In this case, the size appeared quite shiny against the black of the stool and so I could tell which areas I had covered. If the original finish had been a shiny gloss, it would have been harder to tell. Leave the size for at least 12 hours to set.

2. Take some transfer gold leaf (in this case, Versailles) which comes on a sheet attached to a piece of backing paper. When gilding intricate moldings, it is a good idea first to cut the gold leaf into strips the width of the moldings; this makes the leaf easier to handle and is more economical; you use only what you need.

3. Bandage the strip or sheet of gold leaf around the molding, pressing quite hard with the sides of your thumbs or fingers against the backing paper. The gold leaf will stick to the size and leave the backing paper behind. Make sure that you press equally hard against the edges and corners of the moldings, but avoid using your nails which will tear the gold leaf and scratch the size.

4. Don't worry if the gold doesn't stick at first to some tiny areas of the moldings. You can either leave these to create an impression of faded glory or go back over them with the gold leaf (it doesn't matter if one layer of gold leaf sticks to another). If the reason that the gold leaf is not sticking to a few tiny areas is because you missed them when applying the size, you can, as an emergency measure, apply a little gloss varnish to them. The gloss varnish will become tacky within about 10 minutes and you can then apply the gold leaf in the same way.

6. You may feel that the gold is now so new and shiny that it looks out of keeping with the slightly aged, black background. In this case, you should tone it down or distress it to take away some of the sheen, to add depth and to make it look richer and older. However, an oil-based tinted varnish such as those that I have used elsewhere in the book would deaden the luster of the gold. You should use gouache instead to create a watery, translucent mixture through which the gold will glow brightly. Mix some burnt umber gouache with a few drops of water and a drop of detergent which will help the paint adhere to the oily, gilded surface (parchment size is an alternative medium to detergent but there is the inconvenience of heating it to the right temperature in a double boiler). Apply the mixture lightly but unevenly with a No. 5 sable brush so that it collects around the tops and bottoms of the moldings, giving the impression of years of use. The object will dry within about an hour.

5. Rub the object quite gently with a dry rag to remove surplus flakes of gold and to give the gilding a shine. Fold the rag, dip it in some mineral spirits and, with your thumb or finger tip pressed into the back of the fold, wipe around the edges of the gilded moldings. There's nothing that betrays gilding more than stray flakes of gold. Don't touch the moldings themselves because the mineral spirits will remove the oil gilding. Use a cotton swab dipped in mineral spirits for any very intricate moldings.

HANDY HINTS

You often find that the intensity of color varies from area to area around an old piece of painted furniture—fading, for example, around the top through exposure to sunlight or around the handles through heavy use. You may, therefore, need to mix several pots of color, pouring them onto a plate and using more or less of each.

Distressed and Gilded Trug

Time: 4 hours spread over 5 days.

Getting ready: Pour some flat white paint into a cup and thin with mineral spirits to a milky consistency. Brush this onto the surface of the trug with a ½ inch decorator's brush in order to raise the grain of the wood. It is a good idea to cover the table with newspaper because the mixture is very thin and tends to spray everywhere. Then rub down with sandpaper. Smear fine-surface filler into any holes or cracks in the wood and then sand it flush with the surface. Apply one coat of white semigloss, tinted a pale bluey gray with black and ultramarine, and leave to dry overnight.

STEP-BY-STEP RECIPE

1. Mix a sticky glaze the consistency of cream, consisting of:
- 2 teaspoons of varnish
- a teaspoon of flat white
- ½ in. squeeze of raw umber
- ¼ in. squeeze of lemon chrome
- a little under ¼ in. squeeze of black
- a little mineral spirits

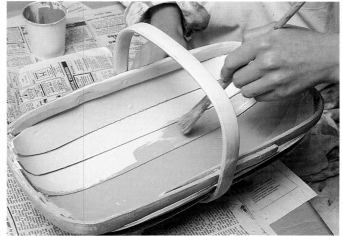

2. Apply the glaze quite roughly to one of the surfaces of the trug with a No. 10 fitch brush, following the grain of the wood.

3. When you have covered some of the surface, try to rub the glaze away with a rag. Because of the varnish, the glaze will dry quite quickly; you want to rub it once the glaze has begun to set but before it has dried to the point at which it will not come off. Rub the surface quite firmly in the direction of the grain. The aim of this technique—known as distressing—is to create the impression that, over the years, dust and dirt, as represented by the browny gray glaze (step 1), have collected in the less exposed nooks and crannies whereas the more exposed areas, as represented by the semigloss undercoat, have been kept clean by use. Rub less vigorously in some places than in others to further the illusion that the finish has been created by age rather than by design. In any case, you will notice that the glaze collects in cracks in the wood and in contours of the grain. Leave to dry for about 6 hours.

4. Apply 12-hour gold size to the handle, the top rim and the feet of the trug with a No. 6 sable brush. Because you didn't paint these areas yellow, hold the trug up to the light so that the size shines and shows which areas you have covered and which you have missed. Leave to dry overnight.

HANDY HINTS

If—as in the case of the trug—you haven't applied a yellow background first, you will have to be more careful when applying the gold leaf.

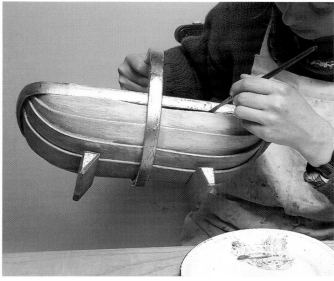

7. On a plate, mix a rich browny gold consisting of:
- a drop of detergent
- a little water
- a tiny squeeze of burnt umber gouache
- a tiny squeeze of black gouache

5. Cut a sheet of Versailles gold leaf into strips approximately the width of the sized areas—the top rim, the handle and the feet. Lay the gold leaf onto the surfaces and press with your finger tips against the back of the transfer paper. Make sure that the strips of gold leaf reach right around the handle and the rim. Use a cotton swab for intricate areas. Leave the gold leaf for about half an hour.

6. Wipe the gilded surfaces with a dry rag. Then, with a rag and mineral spirits, remove any flakes that have strayed over the edges.

8. Apply the mixture with a No. 5 sable brush. This will tone down the brightness of the gold leaf, making it warmer and older in appearance. Don't worry about the little bubbles on the surface; these will add texture to the gold.

GLOSSARY OF DECORATING TERMS

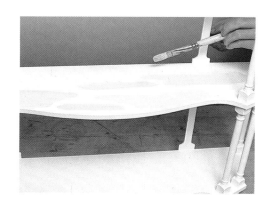

ANTIQUING
The technique of giving a look of age to a newly painted object, achieved by applying a darker tinted glaze or varnish and then partially rubbing it off. See also DISTRESSING.

BADGER SOFTENER
A large, soft, bushy brush that, when drawn gently over a wet glaze, gives it a blurred effect. It is very useful for marbling techniques.

BEADING
A decorative feature consisting of a line of small beads. It is achieved by picking out a series of dots and then highlighting the center of each with a touch of contrasting color.

BIEDERMEIER
German furniture of this period – the first half of the 19th century – is characterized by the use of light-colored woods and a solid design. It now looks surprisingly modern.

BURNT SIENNA
One of the earth colors. A very strong, rich, red pigment often used in coral and terracotta glazes.

BURNT UMBER
A chocolate-brown earth color, often used when creating a glaze for dark wood grains.

CADMIUM SCARLET
A bright red pigment of medium strength, often used to create shades of peach, orange or deep red.

CAPITAL
The upper part of a column, supporting the entablature.

CHINOISERIE
A European decorative fashion of the 17th and 18th centuries, based on an imitation of Chinese artistic motifs. It was widely applied to furniture, tableware, textiles and interiors.

CLASSICAL
A style of architecture and design influenced by the art of ancient Greece and Rome. It is governed by the rules of proportion in that the parts are related both to each other and to the whole.

COLUMN
An upright cylindrical post or pillar with a base at the bottom and a capital at the top.

CONCAVE
A hollow or inward curve.

CONVEX
A rounded or outward curve.

CRIMSON
A deep, luxurious, purple red. It is a weak pigment, however, and when mixed with other colors, it deepens and softens their impact.

DADO RAIL
The molding that separates the lower part of an interior wall from the upper part. Each section of wall is usually decorated in a different way.

DECORATOR'S BRUSH
These are heavy-duty brushes, ranging in width from ½ inch to 4 inches; they are used for undercoating, glazing and varnishing large objects.

DISTRESSING
Similar to antiquing, distressing is the process of making an object appear much older than it is by applying and then rubbing away a partially dried varnish.

DRAGGING
The rearrangement of a wet glaze with a brush to produce fine straight lines.

EARTH COLORS
Shades of brown, ranging from green, yellow and red to dark brown. These are fundamental to woodgraining and marbling and give an instant impression of age and authority when added to a glaze.

EMPIRE
An early 19th-century, French neoclassical decorative style.

ENTABLATURE
The part of a classical order above the columns, consisting of an architrave, a frieze and a cornice.

FAN BRUSH
A brush with bristles that are splayed out in a fan. Fan brushes are used for wood-graining since, when pulled lightly over a wet glaze, the bristles leave grain marks on the wood.

FAUX
A French term meaning "false," as in "faux bois" (wood-graining), "faux marbre" (marbling) or "faux bois clair" (a light-colored wood-grain).

FEATHERS
These make the most delicate, natural brushes there are; their fine tips are used for applying veins to marble. Choose goose or turkey feathers with the sharpest tips.

FERRULE
The metal band or bracket around a paintbrush which keeps the bristles in place.

FILLER
A quick-drying paste used to fill small cracks or holes in the surface of a wall or a piece of furniture before painting.

FILLET
A narrow, flat strip which lies between two moldings.

FLAT FITCH
A good quality, resilient bristle brush, most often used in sizes No. 8 or No. 10, for undercoating and glazing small objects.

FLAT WHITE
A white paint used both as an undercoat and as a medium for a glaze. When applied as an undercoat on wood, it raises the grain and prepares the object for sanding.

GEORGIAN
A term loosely applied to English decorative styles of the 18th century.

GESSO
A mixture of plaster of Paris and size which is modeled onto furniture and moldings prior to water-gilding. It was most commonly used in the Middle Ages and Renaissance to prepare panels or canvas for painting and gilding.

GILDING
The process of decorating with gold leaf. Gold leaf comes in books of very thin sheets and can be bought in a variety of different shades, from acid yellow to bronze. The gold leaf is applied to the object by rubbing it – gold face down – and then peeling away the backing paper. The process of water-gilding, on the other hand, uses a water-based size and loose sheets of gold leaf that are not attached to backing paper. This process is infinitely more complicated and time-consuming.

GLAZE
A thin coat of translucent color, which can be rearranged with a brush to create a variety of effects on the surface of an object.

GOLD LEAF
See also GILDING. Tissue-thin sheets of gold that are either backed with paper for transfer-gilding or left as loose leaf for water-gilding. Both types of gold leaf may be used for decorating furniture or woodwork.

GOOSE FEATHER
See FEATHERS.

GOUACHE
Also known as body color, this paint consists of watercolor pigments and white bound together with gum. Gouache can be used as part of an alternative method for distressing gold leaf.

GRAIN
The pattern and texture of wood that indicate the direction in which it has grown. If you cut wood across the grain, the result will be a rough surface that can never be sanded smooth. Leather and stone can also be said to have a grain.

GRANITE
A light-colored, coarse-grained stone which is widely used for its durability in building.

HB PENCIL
A symbol on British pencils, denoting a medium-hard lead. HB stands for Hard Black.

2H PENCIL
A pencil with a harder lead, which gives a very light line when marking out.

INLAY
A pattern composed of wood, ivory, shell or metal set flush with the surface of wooden furniture.

IVORY
A cream-colored, fine-grained substance derived from elephant tusk or horn. Ivory is often used as an inlay on furniture.

JAPANNING
An imitation, oriental, black lacquer that can be painted onto metal and wooden furniture. See LACQUER.

JARDINIERE
A decorated vessel, made of metal or wood, for holding a flowerpot. Jardinieres are sometimes known as cache-pots.

KEY
Roughening the surface with sandpaper before applying a glaze gives the paint a key on which to adhere.

LACQUER
An oriental varnish which gives a hard, glossy, waterproof finish. It has been widely copied in the West.

LAPIS LAZULI
A brilliant blue semiprecious stone composed of tiny multicolored fragments compacted together. Lapis lazuli is the source of the pigment ultramarine and is used in small ornaments and as an inlay for marbles.

LEMON CHROME
A strongly pigmented, all-purpose yellow, which creates a cooling effect when mixed with most other pigments.

LINING OUT
The process of painting narrow lines in a color that contrasts with the background in order to emphasize existing features, or to invent new ones, on furniture and walls.

LINSEED OIL
The addition of linseed oil to a glaze delays the drying process and keeps the glaze "open," or workable, for longer.

MAHOGANY
A hard, dark, reddish brown wood much used in furniture making.

MALACHITE
A brilliant green mineral found in copper veins. It is often carved to produce small ornaments and then polished.

MAPLE
A light-colored, close-grained wood used mainly for furniture and floors.

MARQUETRY
A decorative effect used on furniture, consisting of a pattern of inlaid wood, brass, shell or ivory veneers. The technique became very popular in France in the late 16th century.

MASKING TAPE
An adhesive tape used to protect the surfaces surrounding an area to be painted.

METAL PRIMER
This protects the surface of metal objects from rust by sealing it from moisture. For surfaces that are already rusty, use a rust transformer – a primer which removes rust.

MINERAL SPIRITS
A colorless solvent used to dilute and thin glazes. It is also used for cleaning brushes and for wiping a wet glaze from painted surfaces.

MITER
A 90 degree joint between two pieces of material, usually wood, formed by the end of each piece being cut at an angle of 45 degrees.

MOLDING
An ornamental strip of wood, stone or plaster which is set into (concave), or projects from (convex), a surface.

MOTIF
A pattern composed of a recurring shape or design.

OBELISK
A stone pillar with four sides, tapering to a pyramidal top. Obelisks were originally erected in pairs at the entrances of ancient Egyptian temples.

OIL COLORS AND STAINERS
Oil-based paints are tough and easy to work with. In this book, I have used ten basic oil colors to achieve a wide range of shades. It is better to combine oil colors with a medium of either white paint or varnish, rather than to use them on their own (which tends to give an uneven, streaky finish and make the drying time longer).

OPEN
The term used to describe a glaze in its workable state. Glazes can be kept "open" for longer with the addition of linseed oil.

ORMOLU
A gold-colored alloy of copper, tin or zinc often used as an ornament on the borders or edges of pieces of furniture. Ormolu was first produced in France in the 17th century and became popular in the 18th and 19th centuries.

PAINT BUCKET
A container looking like a flowerpot with a handle, used for mixing paints.

PANEL
A bordered, rectangular section of a wall, door or piece of furniture.

PEDESTAL
The base upon which a column rests.

PICKING OUT
The technique of emphasizing moldings by painting or gilding them in a color that contrasts with the background.

PIGMENT
A substance, such as a mineral, that occurs naturally and, once ground into powdered form, gives a paint its color.

PINE
The soft wood of the evergreen, resinous pine tree, pine is the cheapest wood available and is often used for flooring. It is usually cut into narrow planks.

PRIMARY COLOR
One of the colors – red, yellow or blue – from which all the other colors are derived.

PRIME
To prepare the surface for sanding and, subsequently, for painting by applying a thin layer of paint or size to raise the grain.

RAGGING
The use of a crumpled rag to rearrange a wet glaze, leaving a rough textured pattern on the surface.

RAILS
The horizontal lengths of timber surrounding a panel. *See* STILES.

RAW SIENNA
A golden, sandy-brown earth color, useful for creating pale wood and yellow marble.

RAW UMBER
A cool, green-brown earth color used to tone down the brightness of white or other colors.

REBATE
A square-edged channel surrounding a panel of wood.

RECESS
A niche or space set back from the surface.

REGENCY
An early-19th-century neoclassical style, equivalent to the Empire period and style in France.

REPEAT
A complete unit of design in a recurring pattern.

RETURN
The edge of a strip or surface, normally set at 90 degrees.

RINGS
The bands separating sections of bamboo, which delineate one season's growth from the next.

SABLE BRUSH
The finest and most expensive brush available. It is made of fine, dark brown sable hair and is used for detailed work.

SANDING
The process of smoothing a surface with sandpaper, in preparation for painting.

SANDPAPER
A heavy-duty paper, coated with sand or an abrasive material, for smoothing down surfaces before painting. Sandpaper comes in varying degrees of abrasiveness, the lightest being flour sandpaper for very delicate work.

SCALLOP
A curved shape, either concave or convex, derived from the shape of a scallop shell.

SCALPEL
A surgical or craft knife with a fine, thin, very sharp blade.

SEMIGLOSS
A paint with a sheen halfway between flat white and gloss. It is easily tinted with oil colors and gives a good surface for subsequent glazing.

SIZE
A thin, gelatinous mixture used to seal or fill surfaces prior to painting or gilding.

SPATTER
The technique of spraying a thin coating of paint onto an object by pulling a finger through the bristles of the brush.

SPINE
The ridge which extends vertically from the ring of a bamboo cane.

SPLAT
The thin upright in the center of the back of a chair.

SPONGING
A cloudy effect achieved by rearranging a wet glaze on a surface with a sponge.

STENCIL BRUSH
A brush with short, stubby bristles used to pounce paint through a stencil.

STENCILING
The process of applying a repeating pattern onto a surface. A design is cut into a stiff card, called the stencil, and this is then positioned onto the surface to be decorated. Using a stencil brush, paint is then pounced through the stencil patterns. The stencil is then carefully lifted away and repositioned so that the pattern can be repeated.

STILES
The vertical parts of a wooden frame or panel.

STIPPLING
An effect created by pouncing a wet glaze with a flat, stiff-bristled brush. The ends of the bristles leave the impressions of tiny dots.

STRINGING LINES
Thin bands of metal or wood that are inlaid or painted onto furniture in order to panel out the surface.

SWAG
An ornamental loop of fruit, flowers or ribbons, often painted onto objects or molded around old fireplaces and ceilings.

TOLE OR TOLEWARE
Tinware that has been painted and decorated to imitate lacquer or enamel.

TORTOISESHELL
The translucent, golden brown outer layer of the hawksbill turtle, used for making jewelry and ornaments. It can very effectively be imitated.

TROMPE L'OEIL
Literally, "to deceive the eye"; making a flat surface appear three-dimensional by painting in shadows and highlights.

TRUG
A shallow, oblong garden-basket composed of thin wooden strips.

ULTRAMARINE
A vivid blue, highly prized in medieval painting as it could then only be obtained by grinding semiprecious lapis lazuli into a powder. This made it a rare and valuable color.

UNDERCOAT
The first coat of paint, generally semigloss, applied to a surface once it has been primed and sanded. The undercoat should always be paler than the topcoat.

VEINING
The technique of producing irregular lines in a color that contrasts with the background in order to produce a marbled effect. Veining is accomplished most effectively with the tip of a strong feather.

VENEER
A thin layer of fine wood covering the surface of a piece of furniture made from a cheaper wood.

VICTORIAN
A style of decoration in furniture that was typical of Queen Victoria's reign (1837–1901). It is characterized by dark colors and heavy, elaborate ornamentation.

VIRIDIAN
A bright, vibrant green.

WATER-GILDING
See GILDING.

WOOD-GRAINING
The technique of painting an imitation wood onto a surface, using a glaze that generally includes one or more of the earth colors.

INDEX